Developing Safety Skills with Young Children

Developing Safety Skills with Young Children

A Commonsense, Nonthreatening Approach

Diana E. Comer

Delmar Publishers Inc.®

Delmar Staff

Associate Editor: Karen Lavroff
Production Editor: Ruth East

For information, address Delmar Publishers Inc.
2 Computer Drive West, Box 15-015
Albany, New York 12212-9985

Printed in the United States of America
Published simultaneously in Canada
by Nelson Canada,
A division of International Thomson Limited

10 9 8 7 6 5 4 3 2 1

Library of Congress Cataloging in Publication Data

Comer, Diana Elizabeth.
Developing safety skills with young children.

Includes index.
1. Safety education—United States. 2. Children's accidents—Prevention—Study and teaching—United States. 3. Child molesting—Prevention—Study and teaching—United States. I. Title.
HQ770.7.C65 1987 649'.1 86-11438
ISBN 0-8273-2668-8 (soft)
ISBN 0-8273-2669-6 (instructor's guide)

To my children and husband for all their support while Mommy researched and wrote this book.

To all the children that need to learn how to be safe and how to tell people if they are not safe so they can grow up enjoying the full promise of childhood.

To Joan, my friend.

CONTENTS

Preface xi
Acknowledgments xiii

INTRODUCTION / Basic Normal Child Development 1

1 / Designing a Comprehensive Safety Curriculum 7

Safety and Protection of Young Children 7
Societal Changes Affecting Child Safety 9
Children's Perceptions of Reality 11
First Aid Instruction Materials 13
Methods for Teaching about Safety 13
Basic Premises of This Child Safety Program 25
General Objectives for the Content Areas within This Safety Curriculum 26
General Objectives for the Adult Using This Program 27
Questions for Review 32

2 / Feeling Good About Me 33

Objectives 33
Curriculum Content 36
Words and Phrases That Help Build Positive Self-Concepts 44
Questions for Review 46

3 / First Aid and My Teddy Bear 47

Basic First Aid 47
Dental Concerns and Nutrition 60
Questions for Review 70

4 / Home Safety 71

Safety in the Home 71
House Safety Tour 80
Dangerous Plants 82
Common Household Poisons 84
Lead Poisoning Update 85
Quick Ways to Childproof the Home 87
Infant and Toddler Equipment Guides 90
Toy Safety and the Young Child 91
Outdoor Playground Safety Rules 92
Commonsense Safety Rules for the Preschool and Day-Care Center 94
Good Sports Sense for the Young Athlete 96
Questions for Review 98

5 / Street Smarts 99

Traffic Safety 99
Stranger Safety 104
The Police 113
Automobile Safety 114
Points to Ponder about Stranger Danger 115
Tips for Children When Walking 117
Questions for Review 118

6 / Victimization Prevention 119

Children's Rights 120
Five Senses 120
Sexual Victimization 135
Review Activities 145

Victimization 149
Adult Responsibilities 160
Indicators of Neglect and Abuse 162
Child Sexual Abuse Fact Sheet 163
Signs of Possible Drug Abuse in Young Children 165
Children's Rights about Victimization Prevention 166
Key Words for Parents 166
Uncle Harry and Amy 167
Questions for Review 169

7 / Parent, Teacher, and Community Relations 170

Communication 174
Children's Rights: An Important Issue 175
Tackling the Problem 176
The Need for Safety Education 180
Ten Ways to Bridge the Communication Gap Between Parents and Children 181
Time-Out Tips for Parents Under Stress 182
Ways That Kids Tell Someone They Need Help 184
Lifesaver Emergency Alert Cards 184
A Quick Check for Your Child's Safety 185
What to Look for in a Good Day-Care Center or Preschool Program 186
How to Choose Good Materials about Abuse and Children 189
Reviews of Some Resources for Teachers and Parents 190
Hot Line Telephone Numbers 193
Audio-Visual Resources for the Teacher 194
Health and Safety Resources 197
National Sources of Sexual Abuse Information and Help 198
Local Sources of Help and Information 199
Questions for Review 200

Bibliography 201
Index 205

PREFACE

Our society has changed vastly during the past thirty years. It has moved from stable home environments and neighborhoods—from a society that was united in concepts of morality and child rearing—to a society that is throwing away the old ideas and experimenting with new and various concepts of morality and life—to changed nuclear family styles. We are now in a madras stage of social development compared to the more black-and-white morality and life found in the past fifty years.

If the rules have changed—if there is no consensus of right and wrong—then we are all engaged in a new and exciting struggle to find or create new rules, guidelines, and paths to a better society. This ongoing struggle is changing our society daily.

Our ideas of what consistutes family and society are changing. Today, *family* can mean a nonmarried single parent; a two-parent family; an extended family; a single-parent family through death, divorce, or separation; or a reassembled family brought together when single parents remarry; and many more types of combinations. Thirty years ago, many Americans still thought in terms of mom, dad, and the children, with perhaps a grandparent or two, as the norm or definition of family. This is just one example of many changes occurring today. If one adds together all the sociological and economic changes, the result is a dramatic change in life-style for most children and also a dramatic change in our perceptions of childhood.

Although people probably have retained the same goal as their parents—of raising happy, well-adjusted, healthy, and successful children—their attitudes toward and means to attain this goal have changed dramatically with the parallel sociological changes. The shift to two working-parent households has meant and will continue to mean a growing need for child caretakers during the critical stages of children's development. There will be more need to increase communication among parent and child and caretaker than in the past when a definition of a parenting role usually meant that the parent knew what was happening because one parent was almost always at home.

Changing neighborhoods have also led to a change in our concept of neighborhood. *Neighborhood* once meant a community, a group of people known to all who collectively provided an extended sense of security for each others' family within the general area. With these and other changes, our systems for child protection have disappeared. We need to fill in the gaps, tighten the loops, and find a new path to protect our children from things, people, and situations that threaten their health, safety, and lives in today's world.

The need to begin teaching our children basic survival skills thus is great. Children need to be taught in nonthreatening and in age-appropriate manners the skill that will help them make them safe physically, will increase their sense of psychological security, and will develop strong feelings of self-confidence, thus helping them meet the challenges of this rapidly changing society in positive and competent ways. Wrapped in our own struggles with the changing mores, we adults need to remember that our children are our most valuable resource and need our attention now. The children are the best of us—our future; they will represent the best or worst of our new society.

Since the choice is ours for a better tomorrow for our children, our goal is to find positive solutions to the problem of their safety. This curriculum offers balanced training for children and families to meet that challenge.

To increase the safety factor for all children, we need to prove that there is a need for safety skill training and that there are positive ways to fulfil this need. We need to set guidelines for who should do this training and how it can be presented in nonthreatening and age-appropriate ways. For training to be successful, it cannot occur in a vacuum. We need to counteract the former neglect of this vital area by educating our teachers, community workers, medical personnel, and parents now. We need to forge a combined approach from which we can change our legal system and our society's perspective about young children to provide them the full protection of the Constitution that is due to all United States inhabitants, especially the children.

ACKNOWLEDGMENTS

The following people have generously helped me complete this effort at safeguarding young children. I want to publicly thank them for their ongoing support and concern for the well-being of children.

Richard M. Dumphy, photographer, Worcester, Mass.

Dr. Bruce Fieldman, pediatric dentist, Worcester, Mass.

Mr. and Mrs. Billy Fontana (Geppetto's Toys, South Street Seaport, New York, N.Y.), friends and suppliers of George the Monkey, who has helped me train people about safety. George is a terrific puppet.

Yvonne Lutter, CAT Program, Worcester, Mass.
Elaine Derry, Camp Fire Girls, Worcester, Mass.

Janet Warren, Girl Scout Council, Worcester, Mass.

Polly Fairservice, Joan Brady, Sue Billings, Jim Baxter, Department of Social Services, Worcester, Mass.

Eleanor Higginbottom, Norton Company, Worcester, Mass.

Jospeh DeFazio, Cambridge College, Northampton, Mass.

Natalie Maynard, American Red Cross, Worcester, Mass.

Pat Glasburg, Mr. and Mrs. Dill, Mrs. Seale, Hahnemann Hospital, Worcester, Mass.

The members of the Worcester Council for Children

The members of the Worcester Business and Professional Women

The faculty and administration of Becker Junior College, Leicester, Mass.

Everyone at Webster Square Day Care Center, Worcester, Mass.

The members of the Worcester Area Association for the Education of Young Children

My friends and neighbors

Sandy Gottsegen, Office for Children, Worcester, Mass.

Leicester Police Department, Leicester, Mass.

Leicester Fire Department, Leicester, Mass.

Worcester Police Department, Worcester, Mass.

Karen Lavroff, Associate Editor, Delmar Publishers Inc.

INTRODUCTION

Basic Normal Child Development

It is important to note that these basic guides are just that. Children do not all grow at the same pace or in the same manner. However, a person working with or parenting young children should understand basic characteristics of children at various stages of development. This knowledge is particularly helpful when trying to draw children into the role play and "what-if" discussions that facilitate learning safety skills.

The Three Year Old

- *Physical* Gaining greater motor activity . . . improved coordination . . . more vigorous and boisterous than two . . . like to play with large blocks . . . and equipment . . . more skillful with their hands.
- *Emotional* More cooperative and like to conform . . . still have difficulty handling emotional energy and still have temper tantrums . . . but less frequently. . . . Because they are curious they can become unintentionally destructive.
- *Intellectual* . . . understand simple questions, statements, and directions. . . . Abstract words are beyond their understanding. . . . Rhythm, repetition and humor please them.
- *Interpersonal* . . . a desire to please . . . beginning to share and take turns. . . . Mother is the favorite companion . . . look to her for security, recognition, and encouragement.

The three-year-old is more skillful with his or her hands. Coloring is a favorite activity for a quiet time of day.

The Four Year Old

- *Physical* . . . noisier, stormier and speedier . . . they hit, jump up and down. . . . Destructive action . . . fully intentional now . . . more skilled in motor activities—all at breakneck speed . . . like to throw balls, cut, saw, lace, color and build with small blocks.
- *Emotional* . . . not too concerned with the feelings of others. . . . Sometimes praise themselves with bragging . . . like to pursue their own course.
- *Intellectual* . . . constantly ask questions . . . imagination is limitless and what they tell is a mixture of truth and fiction . . . fun with imaginary friends . . . dislike repetition. Dramatization of simple stories, group singing . . . and informational material delights them.
- *Interpersonal* "No, I won't!" is the order of the day for four-year-olds . . . defiant but want to be like others in their group . . . like to talk on the phone . . . may become very silly . . . call people names . . . may become very bossy.

The four-year-old likes to play with blocks and loves mixtures of truth and fiction in creative play.

The Five Year Old

- *Physical* ... poised and controlled ... swing, climb, jump and skip with dexterity ... busily engage in purposeful activity ... riding ... toys are satisfying ... fascinated by puzzles and tools.
- *Emotional* ... more conservative in action ... extremely interested in home activities and like to help. ... Babies are of great interest ... can become anxious about whether mother will be home when they leave school.
- *Intellectual* ... still factual and literal ... not interested in the unreal or impossible stories ... may be slow in action but they are persistent.
- *Interpersonal* ... friendly but shy with strangers ... like best to play with other five-year-olds ... want to be good but can't always differentiate right from wrong. When something goes wrong, they may blame the nearest person.

The five-year-old is more poised and controlled and can do more enthusiastic and involved physical activities.

The Six Year Old

- *Physical* ... marked physical growth ... body is out of proportion to muscular control ... may cause awkward and clumsy behavior ... eye-hand coordination is not well-established ... constantly moving whether sitting or standing ... wiggle and squirm.
- *Emotional* ... feelings ... from one extreme to another ... express it with vim and vigor ... still anchored to home and are full of inconsistencies.... They want to be independent yet dependent ... can't make decisions as easily ... like new things ... enthusiastic.
- *Intellectual* ... "Why?" ... ask questions and may try to answer them without help ... beginning to see the connection between spoken and printed word ... vocabulary is concrete ... little concept of time and space ... interest span lengthening ... [like] stories that are real and enjoy having them told over and over.

The six-year-old is constantly moving. He or she is enthusiastic about new things, like learning to ride a bicycle.

- *Interpersonal* . . . beginning to be concerned about social approval . . . early stages of gang formation . . . may hit . . . to attract attention . . . like to tease . . . want to be "it" and want to be in a group . . . seldom want to give up their place . . . usually best friends are of their own sex.[1]

1. Betty L. Broman, *The Early Years in Childhood Education*, second edition (Boston: Houghton Mifflin Company, copyright 1982), 65–68. Used with permission.

CHAPTER 1

Designing a Comprehensive Safety Curriculum

SAFETY AND PROTECTION OF YOUNG CHILDREN

Teachers, parents, and community leaders should teach and role play with young children the basic safety procedures to decrease the child's vulnerability to physical abuse, sexual victimization, and accidents at home and away in a positive, nonthreatening manner that gives children the skills to handle and avoid potentially dangerous situations.

The past thirty-five years have given me the opportunity to be a child, grow to adulthood, and return to working with children as a parent and a teacher. This time has provided the education, insights, and experience to be aware of the problems involved in creating a safe environment for children from various perspectives.

As a teacher of both kindergarten and pre-school-aged children, I have seen children's concerns for their own safety and have had the opportunity to discuss and work through problem areas and concerns with parents. In my present position as the early childhood coordinator at Becker Junior College, Leicester, Massachusetts, I have researched, designed, and implemented a teacher-training program for the preschool level and directed the lab school. An important part of any curriculum development in our program is working with families and their concerns when designing the student teacher's teaching format and content material. A concern parents always raise is the safety of their children.

How is the school going to address this issue? How can we as parents handle this issue? How do you talk to young children about all these safety concerns without frightening them? The need to answer these questions is a valid concern for every school.

Community work offers the opportunity to see and deal with the problems of society and children on a broader spectrum. The Greater Worcester Council for Children is a citizen-based advocacy group that actively looks at children's issues from birth to adulthood. The group works on supporting programs, investigating programs, lobbying for bills that support children's rights, and other aspects of children's needs. The Worcester Area Association for the Education of Young Children, The Worcester Business and Professional Women's Association, Scouting, and PTO work all expose me to a wide variety of community programs and needs. Safety is a recurring theme with most people, whether in discussing camping programs, women's feelings about the safety of parking and walking alone, or how to keep an eye on a large group of children when on a trip. The subject of safety needs to be addressed more in positive terms and with real solutions than with continued rhetoric.

The experience that has best prepared me and most inspired me to help train young children, has been my own experience as wife and mother. Raising five children focuses attention on everything that is going on, from baseball to scraped knees to panicked moments when you couldn't find your child in a store because he was hanging on a rack. These and other common parenting experiences have increased my sensitivity and awareness of the problems, fears, guilts, and joys of raising children today. Dr. Muriel Camarra, an eminent social psychologist and a mother of six, discussed parenting in the 1980s at a Citizens Resource Center workshop. She said it is a time for parents and children to grow together. They need to live together with reachable goals—one day at a time.[1] I feel she is in touch with all the societal changes as we are learning and growing together and making our own rules. Our society has changed—the rules, the guidelines, our support systems, and our expectations from life. Think back to your own childhood if you want to see how change is abounding.

My earliest recollections as a child are filled with people. The thoughts make me feel warm inside as I remember sitting on the porch on hot summer nights, walking to the local mom-and-pop store, playing with my friends in the baseball field, sledding on cardboard boxes, and many more activities. I belonged. Everyone knew who I was, who my parents were, and where I lived. The knowledge that I was coming home with wet sneakers preceded me by at least ten minutes through the neighborhood mother network. I knew about strangers, but I don't remember meeting any until I was older. I knew what was expected of me. Parents knew what was expected of them. Society was definite

1. Muriel Camarra, Citizen's Resource Center Workshop, Keynote Lecturer, "Parents and Children Growing Together," University of Massachusetts Medical School, Worcester, Mass., January 21, 1984.

about morality. Perhaps it was an easier time in which to parent and to grow up.

Please note that I said *maybe.* Perhaps it was too protective a time and perhaps we were too coddled. Perhaps that is why so many of my peers had difficulty adjusting to the world of reality in their early adult years. Whatever the reasons and whatever the pros and cons of raising children then or now, society has moved past those days.

SOCIETAL CHANGES AFFECTING CHILD SAFETY

The society in which I am raising my children is different than that in which I was reared. I knew the homes on our street by names, not by numbers. My children do not know the names of everyone who lives on our street. My children went to nursery school to have friends their own age to play with. My children have a working mother. This is a long way from the 1950s. "Today's typical family is no longer the breadwinning father, the housewife mother, and the children. Instead, it consists of two or more wage earners. Furthermore, the family type that has mushroomed the most in recent years is the one headed by a single parent. By 1990 it's expected that only one in every four married women will be a full-time housewife."[2] "By March 1980 43 percent of all children under the age of six had working mothers. . . . Most of the increase in the number of women who work has been among married women with children, the very group who in the past, were considered the least likely to seek outside employment."[3]

Earlier in the chapter, I mentioned the society of the past with its strong support systems and few worries about child rearing. This does not mean that parents did not have any concerns; it is just that their concerns were less urgent and less emphasized than are safety concerns today. Every generation has had some safety rules for children. Children on the way West were told to be wary of snakes, stay near the wagon, and so forth. In more recent times such safety tips as Don't drink from other's glasses! Don't share combs! Don't take medicine from anyone other than mother! Don't play on the third floor porch! were offered by parents. Most of the concerns of the recent past were related to accident and health safety issues. Today, parents are concerned about accident and health safety, but even more so about stranger and people safety issues.

If we define safety as the condition in which children are not in danger either to themselves or from other circumstances or people, we can see what an

2. Sally Wendkos Olds, *The Working Parents Survival Guide* (New York: Bantam Books, 1983), 3.
3. Olds, 4.

awesome task it is to keep children safe. The sources of danger to a child are numerous and change with the society, the times, and our perceptions of what is dangerous. One example of how our sources change is a shopping mall development in a small town. The Jones family live on the quiet street near the main road through town. A mall is built nearby and suddenly their nice, safe street becomes a shortcut to the mall. Now, both children and adults need to learn new skills to adapt to the changed situation.

Dangers a child can self-inflict are poisons, medication overdoses, and inappropriate uses of materials in and out of the house. Dangers from other people are "friendly" strangers, physical abuse, sexual victimization, and molestation. Dangers from circumstances include fire, flood, water in general, accidents, and other instances when a child is at the mercy of the elements with little or no warning. Although these weather-related and accident-related dangers cannot be controlled, skills are needed to react to them.

Are there more dangers today than in the past? What is causing this change in the dangers to which children are exposed each day? To answer these questions, it is necessary to look at the societal changes. This brief review should yield some answers and reveal the need for training in survival skills. Families are radically changing. Even our definition of family is no longer valid. Family, to many people, used to mean mom, dad, children, and grandparents. Today, family can mean a single parent, either through nonmarriage, separation, divorce, or death; two wage-earning parents; or even life on a commune.

The escalating divorce rate has resulted in an increase in single-parent families. "The divorce rate has more than doubled in the past ten years. . . . More than 60 percent of these divorcing couples have children. . . . It is estimated that 20 percent of the children in elementary school have divorced parents. In some of the Kindergarten and First Grade classes, this figure is closer to the 40 to 50 percent level (Wilkinson and Beck 1977)."[4] The job normally done by two parents is now either divided or done by the custody parent. A few decades ago, very few families experienced divorce. Many unhappy couples stayed together for the sake of the children or for social or religious reasons. As the divorce rate has increased, so has social acceptance of divorce. Much of the damage done by a divorce can be minimized if the adults involved support the children and assure them of love and stability. A frightening violation of a child's rights is using a child in a divorce or separation case as an article of revenge. Some good books and articles on divorce are highly recommended. Since child kidnapping often involves a disputed custody situation, kidnapping is covered in the curriculum.

Single parenting has additional stress and problems for the parent. "You don't need a microcomputer to tell you that when one person has to do all the

---

4. Patsy Skeen and Patrick McHenry, "The Teacher's Role in Facilitating a Child's Adjustment to Divorce," *Annual Editions: Early Childhood Education,* ed. Judy Spitler McKee (Guilford, Conn.: Dushkin Publishing, Inc., 1982), 130.

work and caring that is usually shared by two persons, more time and more energy are called for. . . ."[5] It is more difficult to return to work and also to provide parent coverage for the children when only one parent is present.

"In 1981 sixteen million children between the ages of five and thirteen had working mothers, according to a report of the U.S. Department of Labor. There is no going back."[6] The days of stay-at-home parents and Beaver Cleaver are gone. Many single parents need to find quality child care. We thus need to promote more day-care and after-school-care options at affordable costs. With the shortage of affordable settings, we are finding through our Offices for Children and other agencies that more children are being left home alone for part or even for all of the day when the parent works. Statistics are not available, however, because no one wants to admit to leaving a young child home alone because of social censure and because it is illegal. Knowing that many children are home alone, however, it behooves concerned adults to provide the children with skills to be safe at home and on their own.

Mobility within our society has caused another gap in the support system that used to exist for children. Thirty years ago, perhaps one or two mothers in most neighborhoods worked. Thus, many other mothers were around as babysitters or for support. In an emergency, children knew that adults were home next door and who the adults were. Few neighborhoods are that stable today. We do not always get to know our neighbors or trust our children to them. With so many mothers working, there is apt to be no person at home in the neighborhood during the day to cover for the working parent in an emergency.

Another danger to children can be our own attempts at protecting them. If we give children information they cannot understand at their level of development, if we give rules for safety that are firm and unbending, we can be setting them up for tragedy. We need to increase the children's chances of survival by speaking at their level and in their vocabulary. Children do not always mean the same thing by certain words that we adults think them to mean. Children also do not understand that circumstances can change rules.

CHILDREN'S PERCEPTIONS OF REALITY

Jean Piaget observed children playing a game of marbles. "Four to seven year olds just seemed to view rules as an interesting example of social behavior of older children. They did not understand them but tried to go along with them. Piaget concluded that younger children see rules as absolute and external."[7]

5. Olds, 224.

6. Ruth Kramer Baden et al., *School-Age Child Care, An Action Manual* (Boston: Auburn House Publishing Company, 1982), 2–3.

7. Robert F. Biehler, *Child Development: An Introduction*, Second Edition, pp. 464 and 465. Copyright © 1981 by Houghton Mifflin Company. Used by permission.

This observation is one example of a basic problem of which parents and people who work with young children must be aware on a conscious level. What you tell young children, they believe as an absolute and unbending fact or rule. If you tell a child to do everything the babysitter says or do whatever Uncle Harry says, you are setting them up for a possible danger. No, you do not think the babysitter will do anything wrong, but neither did other parents whose children were harmed or victimized by an adult in a trust position. A child will often "go along" even if frightened or uneasy because the trust in the parent is so strong. "The younger child sees rules as real—ready made and external. . . . The letter of the law rather than the spirit of the law must be observed and no exceptions are allowed . . . no allowances made for motives or intention."[8] This differentiation of thinking levels and readiness demonstrates a need to be very specific with young children and to discuss alternatives. The child needs to be aware of when and how to say "no." The child needs to have you, as the basic trust adult, validate his or her right to say "no."

Truth is also a problem for children. Reality is another. Children tend to see things from a different perspective than do adults. Did you speak to a stranger? asks a mother of her three-year-old, having observed her do just that. No, answers the child. Did the child lie? No. The child, on further questioning, reveals that she spoke to the lady. "You know, the one who says 'Hi' everyday when she walks by." Mother had not seen her walk by, but she was no stranger to the child. A friend revealed that her son almost let the garbage man in the house while she was in the shower. He needed to use the telephone. Fortunately, the man waited outside for the child to get mommy, but at his insistence, not the child's. When she asked him why he was going to let a stranger in the house, he replied, "Because he was my friend on the big truck." Children learn literally without understanding nuances and without understanding that changed circumstances can change a response to a situation. A child is told to stay in his room no matter what after his fifth trip to the bathroom. A fire breaks out upstairs. Chances are good that the child will be burned or hurt if he is not prepared to cope with changed circumstances. It is imperative that we communicate with children with a clear understanding of their perceptual abilities and understandings.

Safety and survival skills should be taught by parents, teachers, and community workers. They need to be taught simply. The teachings should be consistent to lessen confusion and thus to increase the child's chances of remembering the skills in an actual situation. The skills need to be taught in a manner that appeals to children, is easy to remember, and demonstrates to the child the importance of both the subject and the instructor's confidence in the child's ability to handle the situation.

This introduction establishes the need for adults who work with young children to teach survival skills. Every parent, teacher, concerned adult, and

---

8. Biehler, 465. Used by permission.

community worker should realize the significance of safety and children's rights. This curriculum addresses preventive solutions to many concerns about safety and young children. We can work together to create a caring, safe environment for all children that affirms their rights as individuals and recognizes their self-competence.

FIRST AID INSTRUCTION MATERIALS

The next few pages are from the American Red Cross BATMAN program (reprinted with permission). The BATMAN program is a first aid and safety program for school-aged children. Training is available from your local Red Cross Chapter and with it this packet of posters and lesson plans. The BATMAN program is especially geared to grades 4, 5, and 6, and it also can be adapted for use by lower grades.

The program is very well done and has a high level of motivation for children. The training posters work well for young children because they are colorful and simple to understand. Shown here are some of the posters available in the kit; they represent the ones that can best be used with young children. The cost is very low for the packet and the training. Check your local Red Cross Chapter about this training and its cost. I can't stress enough the importance of taking Standard Red Cross First Aid and CPR for your own sake. If you work with children, it is especially crucial for you to know what you are doing. One good side benefit in these days of law suits, is that the Red Cross legally backs current Red Cross First Aid card holders if an unforeseen complication arises as long as Red Cross procedures were followed. As a teacher, this is insurance against any hesitancy to act in an emergency. This is also true as a parent whose house is often filled with children's friends.

You never know when first aid training, even with young children, may save a life. Recently in California, a five-year-old and his three-year-old brother saved their mother from drowning in the family pool by knowing how to get help and not panicking. You often are alone with children. What would occur if something unexpected happened to you? Are the children in your care prepared?

METHODS FOR TEACHING ABOUT SAFETY

How does the young child learn best? What "we have learned from the study of young children, especially in recent decades, has forced us to regard the young child as an involved learner who learns best by initiating and actively par-

Children are active learners. They learn best by doing, not just by listening. Can you imagine learning to play baseball by listening to a lecture?

ticipating in learning experiences."[9] "The student in early childhood needs to be an active, involved learner, with real experiences and many concrete materials available to explore and manipulate in the process of cognitive learning."[10] The young child needs to have repetition in learning as well as hands-on experience for best learning and retention. Dramatic play offers both of these opportunities, with the added motivational feature—Fun. "Little children love to pretend when they play . . . children are able to discuss what they are playing or pretend they are someone else talking within the sociodramatic play activity . . . the teacher is a facilitator of dramatic play."[11]

9. Sue Clark Wortham, *Organizing Instruction in Early Childhood* (Newton, Mass.: Allyn & Bacon, Inc., 1984), 8. Used by permission.
10. Wortham, 9. Used by permission.
11. Wortham, 212. Used by permission.

GENERAL DIRECTIONS FOR GIVING FIRST AID

Keep the injured person lying down.  **Do not give liquids to an unconscious person.**  **Restart breathing with mouth-to-mouth artificial respiration.**  **Control bleeding by pressing on the wound.**  **Dilute swallowed poisons**  **and call the Poison Control Center. Keep broken bones from moving.**  **Cover burns with thick layers of cloth.**  **Keep heart-attack cases quiet and give cardiopulmonary resuscitation (CPR) if it is necessary**  **and if you have been trained. Keep a fainting victim lying flat.** 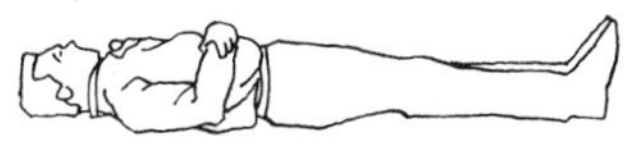

For eye injuries, pad and bandage both eyes.  **Always call a doctor.**

For more information about these and other lifesaving techniques, contact your Red Cross chapter.

FIGURE 1.1
Courtesy of the American National Red Cross.

FIGURE 1.2
Courtesy of the American National Red Cross.

FIGURE 1.3
Courtesy of the American National Red Cross.

DIAL "O"

(911 WHERE USED)

1. SAY: "THIS IS AN EMERGENCY CALL"
2. EXPLAIN EMERGENCY
3. GIVE NAME, ADDRESS, AND TELEPHONE NUMBER
4. DON'T HANG UP!

FIGURE 1.4
Courtesy of the American National Red Cross.

BASIC AID: FALLS

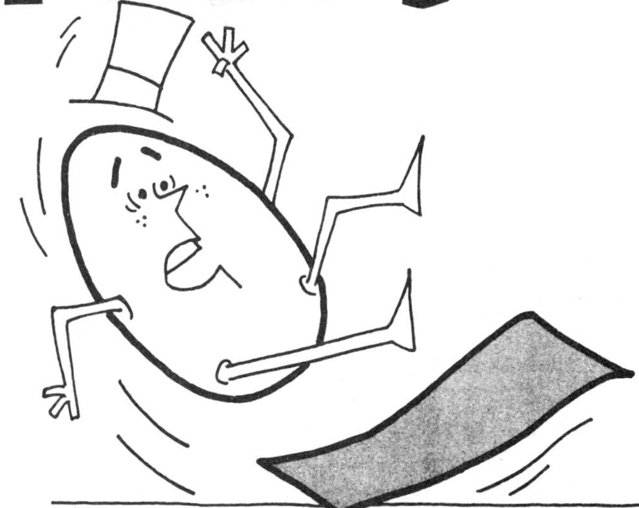

1. DON'T MOVE VICTIM!
2. KEEP VICTIM CALM!
3. GET HELP!

FIGURE 1.5
Courtesy of the American National Red Cross.

SEVERE:

1. HAVE VICTIM LIE DOWN
2. APPLY DIRECT PRESSURE
3. GET HELP!

FIGURE 1.6
Courtesy of the American National Red Cross.

NOSEBLEED

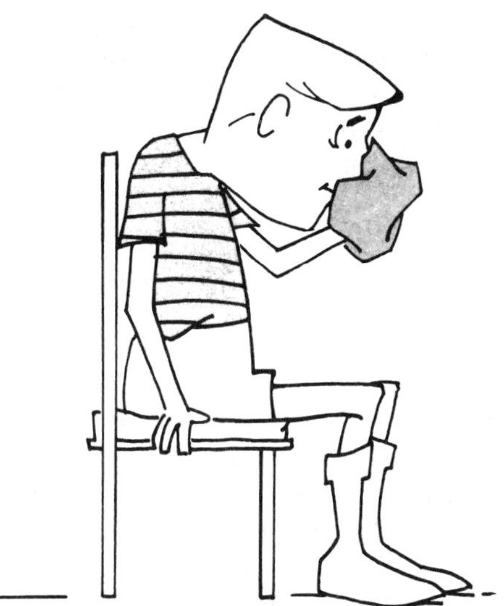

1. SIT DOWN
2. STOP THE BLEEDING

FIGURE 1.7
Courtesy of the American National Red Cross.

As young children strive to be independent and grown up, it makes sense to appeal to this desire when teaching them. The opportunity to consider options and handle situations during dramatic role plays motivates children and facilitates learning. The confidence of role playing potentially dangerous situations and choosing the correct responses, adjusting to new situations correctly, and the sense of mastery developed over situations cannot be underestimated in planning the curriculum for safety with young children.

Role play is also a useful technique to help children change their perspectives about themselves. Physically, children are smaller than most adults or people who could potentially victimize them.

Try to remember when you felt smaller than the people around you. Or, remember when you felt very awkward. Perhaps you were the only one in dress clothes when others were dressed for a football game. Do you remember how dumb or insignificant you might have felt? It is an awful feeling! Children often feel they will never get big; everyone is bigger than they are; they are small and helpless. They depend on adults for food, security, and basic survival. They need to do everything you tell them. No wonder the first word to acclaim personhood is *no!* In this curriculum will be integrated the child's rights, including that of saying *no!*

Another method successful with young children is making books. Even when children cannot read, they enjoy books. There is something grown-up about books. To make your own is special and brings with it interest and retention of whatever is in the book. Making books also provides good reinforcement because an adult can read and reread the book to the child.

Book making and related activities are used to teach children along with music, fingerplays, and sticker reinforcements for reaching goals. Children, particularly young children, need to learn at their own rate; thus, the reinforcements are provided as each child passes each content area rather than at the end of the program.

Children learn better when the learnings make sense, are presented in a progressive order, and contain information that is complete and accurate. The trust younger children give should not be compromised. It is important that whatever facts you give the children be accurate. Granted, the facts must be at a level the children can understand and need not be told in meticulous detail, but there is no reason not to give the facts even to the youngest child.

This curriculum can help adults deal with another difficulty when presenting safety issues to young children—how to present the information in a nonthreatening manner that supports the child's sense of security and emotional well being.

To facilitate a sense of understanding and security within the children with whom this curriculum will be used, the program is set on a progression that emphasizes learnings from known to unknown, or items of high comfort level to those of less comfort. Since the child can progress on an individual level and rate, no child would be forced to handle any subject matter until comfortable with it. The adults will, in fact, have more of a comfort level problem than most children do when discussing and role playing situations. Children are generally open and uninhibited about feelings and emotions when they feel an adult is interested in what they are saying and when they feel secure with that adult.

The adult working with young children will be able to choose how often and for how long to use a particular lesson area. The reasons for this flexibility are obvious to most people who work with young children. The attention span of young children varies so greatly that it would be almost impossible to establish a time sequence. How will you know when to move a child along or how to individualize for a particular group or child? "Essential to adapting and individualizing the program is observation. Teachers evaluate the children's needs and the success of program adaptions to those needs by observing what the children do."[12] Along with the observations of the adult, the program has built in a few clues as to the children's grasp of the learnings.

Since the scope of protection is so vast, the subject is divided into four content areas that progress from most known to least known. These areas include Basic First Aid, General Safety at Home, Street Smarts, and Victimization Prevention. It is recommended that the lessons be used in the order arranged to keep intact the stages of development of trust and understanding.

- Basic First Aid—all about me, my body, and other people
- Home Safety—all about my home, yard, and family
- Street Smarts—all about my street, neighborhood, and outer world
- Victimization Prevention—all about my rights and my safety from more subtle or dangerous sources

After reading through these content areas, it is obvious that one should not talk about sexual abuse without developing trust or leading up to an understanding of this level.

Included in each content area are songs, fingerplays, suggested activities with a group of suggested role plays, and a booklet or papers to reinforce the learnings. Each content area or chapter uses the sticker card as a "report card" of the areas. A sticker will be given as the child completes each level until each child receives all four stickers. The parent or teacher can decide on what kind of reward will be given at the end. The reward can be bringing home the sticker report or a Safe, Strong, and Free Party.

How do the adults present this type of curriculum to children? To help you present the information, read this series of thoughts and keep them in mind as you deliver the curriculum.

---

12. K. Eileen Allen and Betty Hart, *The Early Years; Arrangements for Learning* (Englewood Cliffs, N.J.: Prentice-Hall, 1984), 199.

"Keep the tone of the conversation positive, not threatening; make it informative, not test-like.
Describe the situation and then ask your child how he would respond.
Help direct your child's thinking so that she can arrive at a right answer herself. Don't make her feel bad about a wrong answer but do help her to see what the consequences could be.
Have your child practice using the correct behavior. This is important because many children can explain what they'd do, but cannot actually carry it out."[13]
Limit the number of situations used at a time, keeping in mind the age and developmental readiness of your child or group.
The learning should be fun. Keep it light and gamelike.
"Review four times a year."[14] This will help keep the information and responses fresh and ready to use in an emergency situation.
"Try to keep distractions to a minimum.
Validate the child's feelings. . . . Do not make assumptions about the child's feelings. . . . Acknowledge what s/he is feeling. Reflecting these feelings back to the child affirms their emotions, while demonstrating that, yes, you really are listening.
Always believe the child. Never assume s/he is lying.
Remain calm. When confronted with a crisis situation . . . your reaction makes a difference to the child."[15]

The Children's Awareness Training offered by the Worcester (Massachusetts) Rape Crisis Center and Camp Fire Girls had good suggestions for adults working with young children. When dealing with a long-winded child who wanders off the intended discussion path, do not cut the child off. Acknowledge the child's contribution and then ask if anyone has anything else to contribute about the topic. Another important right to remember is that children should be treated with respect. You do not talk down to people whom you respect. Talking down reinforces the attitude that children have nothing to say and implies they are incapable of thinking for themselves. Understanding the power differential between adults and children is important. Try to present options whenever possible to promote a child's feelings of strength and ability rather than reinforcing feelings of powerlessness. Finally, adults should see the children as problem solvers; this is a cornerstone of teaching prevention of dangers to young children.[16]

---

13. Terri Fields, "Teach Your Kids to Protect Themselves," *Family Circle* (March 6, 1984), 48.
14. Field, 48.
15. Central Massachusetts Camp Fire and Worcester Area Rape Crisis Program and Worcester Area Mental Health, *Children's Awareness Training* (Worcester, Mass. supported by Federal Grant R 18 MH 37549–01, 1982, 1983, 1984), 20.
16. Central Mass. Camp Fire, 24–25.

Some basic premises lie behind the design of this system of teaching safety to young children. Some have already been mentioned, and it is important to look at them as a foundation for building. The adult should be fully aware of the intent and extent of these premises. Accepting them will make this program work for you as a safety trainer of young children.

The building-block approach to safety relies on child confidence and sense of self. As the child becomes more self-assured and capable, the child becomes less likely to be a victim.

Another integral and vital part of this program is parent participation. For this reason many pages are fashioned so they can be easily copied and sent home to parents as information bulletins or newsletter sections. This practice enhances the communication between the school or community program and parents and reinforces the child self-safety aspects with continuity between home and school, or home and group.

Use the sheets in the book or create your own. A neat and perfect package is not needed to teach safety training. All you need is to get the children motivated and involved with common sense and some training basics. Materials you make are as valid to get your points across as are commercially prepared ones. You can use this curriculum as a springboard and add to it with your own experiences and insights.

Before you teach the four safety training areas, a few words about self-concept development are important. This book also contains a final parent-teacher chapter to tie together the whole program and reinforce the importance of the all-important link among school, community, and home. With these aspects in mind, you are now ready to learn how to teach safety to young children.

BASIC PREMISES OF THIS CHILD SAFETY PROGRAM

1. Young children are **capable**!
   They can learn when taught in age-appropriate and interesting ways.
2. Young children can use good **judgment**!
   They can think and use good thinking skills when they learn what to do in a given set of circumstances.
3. Young children should be taught safety through a **building block approach**!
   They best remember, as do we all, information as they are ready to receive it. Preparation for a given topic in a sensible format where the later information builds on former is going to be better remembered.
4. Young children should be taught safety training by **trusted adults in an ongoing manner**!

To have a sex expert or a safety expert walk in and do a day's lesson is not the most effective way to safeguard children or to teach safety because so many questions will come up later. You need someone with whom the children can have an ongoing discussion about the subject and related problems or questions—someone who will **be there**. Further, if the children do not trust the adult involved, it is unlikely they will **ask** for help or **ask** for the answers to the questions that most touch their needs.

5. Safety issues should be handled in **positive and nonthreatening ways**!
   The people who deal with young children about safety issues should know that children need to be made aware **without being frightened**. Do not take away their right and need to believe in people or their need for positive kinds of touch.
6. Young children are best taught through **active participation** because children are **active learners**!
   Young children are very active. Few adults could keep up a full day of doing everything the average youngster does. It makes sense to try to bring across safety training by using a child's **natural learning style**. Therefore, the people who teach young children would make the most effective impact by providing activities that allow movement and a great deal of interaction and involvement.
7. Children are most effectively safeguarded when **parents** are **also actively involved**!
   Since parents are the primary teachers and role models for the young child, their involvement with the trainer (preschool or primary grades teacher) and interest in the program will serve to solidify the learnings about safety. Consistency is important to lessen any misunderstandings and to allow the child to react to an emergency without hesitation. Parents must be invited to come and find out what is being taught and to give input. Making parent involvement part of the reinforcement aspect of the lessons will further strengthen the child's retention of the safety training concepts.

GENERAL OBJECTIVES FOR THE CONTENT AREAS WITHIN THIS SAFETY CURRICULUM

The objective of the curriculum is to prevent the many senseless and needless tragedies that can befall our young children by replacing their ignorance with sound, basic survival skills while supporting their positive self-concepts and feelings of competency in a nonthreatening and caring manner.

At the completion of this program, each child should be able to:

1. Verbalize his or her name, address, and telephone number.
2. Handle basic first aid procedures.
3. Understand and follow basic fire safety procedures, including successfully executing a fire drill.
4. Understand and execute basic water safety rules.
5. Understand and role play basic telephone manners and safety.
6. Understand and role play basic at-home stranger safety, including a trial run with a friend of the parent who is a stranger to the child.
7. Recognize household dangers and how to avoid them.
8. Recognize and respond appropriately to safety hazards both from vehicles and strangers in the street.
9. Recognize their rights as children.
10. Recognize who is a stranger and successfully role play different situations.
11. Create and adapt specific learnings to handle "what if" situations.
12. Execute successfully three self-defense modes (one safety yell and two physical responses to threat).
13. Recognize when, what, and how to communicate to the trusted adult information that has confused or upset the child.
14. Feel safe, strong, and free about himself or herself as a person.
15. Feel comfortable and secure in his or her relationship with parent/s and/or the trusted adult.

GENERAL OBJECTIVES FOR THE ADULTS USING THIS PROGRAM

1. To increase adult awareness of the many dangers to young children.
2. To impress on adults the serious need to promote survival or safety skills development with the young children.
3. To help the adult feel comfortable in disseminating, in a nonthreatening and age-appropriate manner, the needed information to children.
4. To open effective lines of communication between parent and child.
5. To dispel many of the myths about young children in our society.
6. To impress on adults the need for active involvement with the organizations and institutions that are trying to change and promote the rights of children within our changing society.

FIGURE 1.8
Two samples of sticker boards that chart progress.

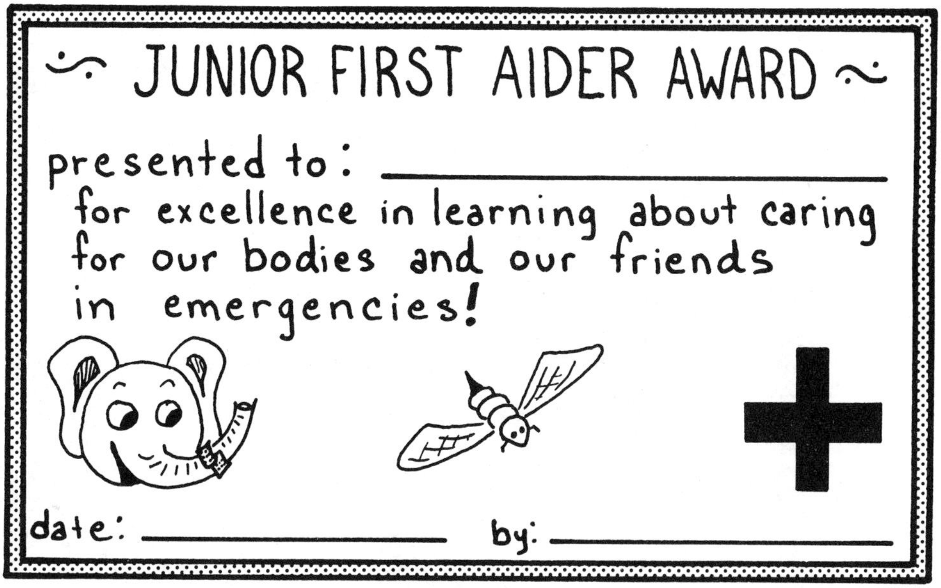
JUNIOR FIRST AIDER AWARD
presented to:
for excellence in learning about caring for our bodies and our friends in emergencies!
date:
by:

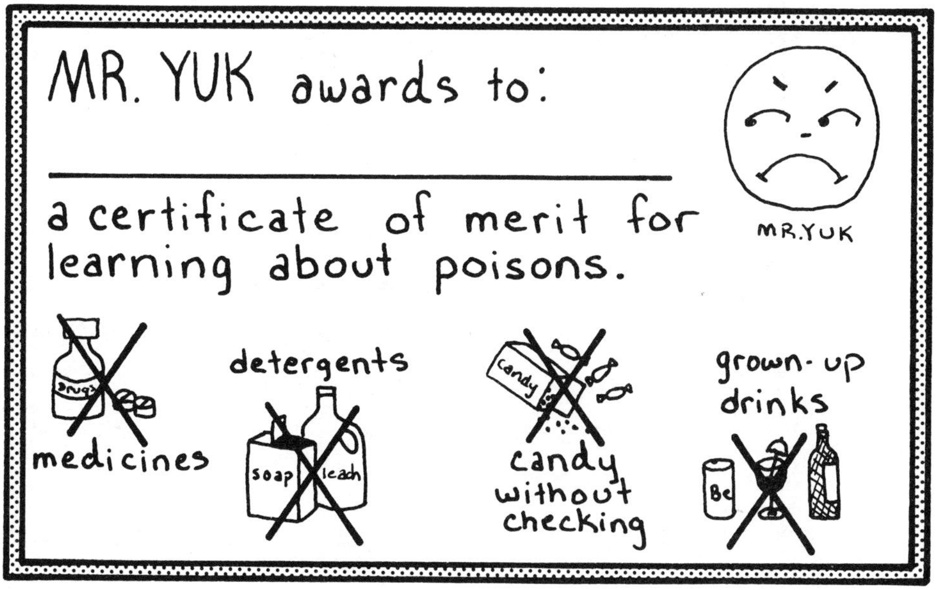
MR. YUK awards to:
a certificate of merit for learning about poisons.
MR. YUK
drugs
medicines
detergents
soap
bleach
candy
candy without checking
grown-up drinks

FIGURE 1.9
Certificate samples.

WINTER

WATER SAFETY PATROL

SUMMER

to: ______________________

I never swim alone!
I never skate alone!
When someone's safety is in doubt,
I don't jump in, I throw help out!

SPRING

by: ______________________

FALL

Be a Super Dooper Snooper!

____

is a great snooper!

Snoopers always practice good telephone safety and door safety at home.
Snoopers never fall for tricks to make them open doors!

signed by: ______________________

Certificate samples.

Certificate samples.

QUESTIONS FOR REVIEW

1. How important is role play in teaching young children?
2. How have our neighborhoods changed, and why is it necessary to teach safety to young children? Give three reasons.
3. How has our definition of family changed?
4. Piaget had some ideas on the difference between adult perceptions and children's perceptions. How do these differences affect how you will teach young children about safety?
5. Safety and survival skill training for young children has to be consistent and simple, yet needs to be taught in a manner that

   a. ____

   b. ____

   c. ____

   and your confidence in the child.
6. What is the BATMAN program?
7. Why should adults take American Red Cross first aid training?
8. How do young children learn best? What methods work well to help children remember?
9. How fast should learning progress? What is this program's timeline?
10. What is the advantage of nonthreatening skill development to the child?
11. What are the four stages or building blocks for teaching safety to young children in this chapter?
12. What tone of voice should the adult use when working with young children?
13. How do you direct the child's learning?
14. How many situations should be used at one time to demonstrate various safety skills?
15. How many times a year should you review the safety training with the young child?
16. How do you deal with a long-winded child who is drifting off the subject?
17. How should adults view children in the problem-solving process?
18. Can you name five objectives of the book in general for the child?
19. Can you name three objectives of the book for adults?
20. How do you use the stickers in this program?

CHAPTER 2

Feeling Good About Me

OBJECTIVES

After working with the material in this chapter, the children will be able to:

1. Recognize what a family is.
2. Develop a sense that they are each special as individuals and as a part of a family.
3. Tell you their name, address, and how to dial home.
4. Tell you and demonstrate facial expressions for the emotions of happy, sad, fear, surprise, and anger.
5. Tell you and demonstrate socially acceptable expressions of these emotions.
6. Begin to understand the rights of children for themselves and those of other people.

In general, before you can teach safety skills children can use, you must lay a foundation of self-confidence and a strong sense of self-worth. Learning about oneself is a strong initial step to the development of a sense of self-worth. Another word more commonly used for these self-realizations is *self-concept. Self-concept* is a sense of how I see myself—my strengths, my weaknesses, my self in comparison with other people. What I think about myself is greatly influenced by what my parents, friends, and society tells me about myself. It is also influenced by my personality and my environment.

Each child has an individual self-concept. Some children are handicapped by a poor sense of self. Even well-meaning parents can contribute to a poor self-concept when they apply stereotypes about children to their own children. We have all seen parents who perpetuate the myths of helplessness and extreme innocence by preventing their children from trying new activities or by keeping their children ignorant about their bodies and social situations. As a result, the children reflect a self-concept that proves they are powerless, fearful, and shy. These children are the most likely to become victims of bullies in peer relations and prey for unscrupulous adults who exploit children physically.

On the positive side, it is not difficult to help children develop a stronger self-concept. Providing an atmosphere that allows children to try new activities and ideas within a safe environment quickly helps the child see that they are strong and capable. These opportunities for children to test themselves are important and need not be formal in setting. They can be as simple as trying and finally climbing a backyard climber, swimming without help, or eating a new vegetable that was never tried before. If you have ever seen a child's face as he or she has accomplished a goal, then you know how important these accomplishments are. By doing for children all the time, you may prevent them from experiencing an important sense of accomplishment. It is also vital that children be allowed to fail without ridicule or undue attention. An adult encouragement that next time it will be easier coupled with a pat on the back for trying will make it easier for a child to try again.

In this building-block approach to self, a child first accomplishes one task successfully or feels personally successful. The child can then go to the next task. Each task builds on the success of the previous one. Each block carefully laid builds a secure foundation for a strong self-concept.

It is important to praise children, but caution is necessary. Empty praise is useless. Praise must be valid to further a child's development. Praise should be specific and honest. Practice until you can say "well-done" in at least 100 ways. Meaningful praise will encourage the child to rise to new challenges. For example, if Molly never tried to fingerpaint because it is messy and she then does try, she should be praised for trying. Molly should not be told that her painting is the greatest if in fact, it is just a first smear. If you tell her it is the best, she will have no reason to do better or be more creative. She probably will realize that you have not told the truth. Real praise will be rendered useless. You might honestly say, "Molly, how wonderful that you tried fingerpainting! What a nice color you chose. Next time, you can try some other colors or another special way of painting. I'm very proud that you tried painting."

To find we are not alone is another confidence builder. Other people have the same fears and problems. Talking about who we are and how we feel is important. Talking gives children the opportunity to tell and share their feelings and, just as important, to listen and hear other children share their feelings. This sharing helps the children to feel they are part of a peer group and also helps them understand that everyone has fears, funny little thoughts, and feel-

Reading is an effective way to reinforce and help the young child distinguish emotions. Older children love to read to younger ones.

ings. They need to know they are not the only ones. Adults should share honestly with children their own feelings, including fears. A child can only benefit from adults who help them realize that emotions are valid and even adults have them. Think how much better a child who is afraid of the dark feels if the parents or teachers admit that when they were younger, they were afraid of the dark, too. Suddenly, the child is not alone! Suddenly, the child is not such a scaredy cat or a baby! After all, if mom was afraid and now she's not, I'll be okay, too!

Children are packages of emotions. Learning what is socially acceptable for the manifestation of these emotions is as vital a part of growing to be a confident and successful adult as is learning to read or program a computer. Education for young children sometimes seems to emphasize academics at the expense of the socialization skills. Sharing and caring are not natural to the young child, as many parents have realized when the joy of their life bites or kicks a neighbor's child. The characteristics of sharing and caring need to be carefully and consistently taught. Adult example is important. Also needed are instruction in the techniques of expressing one's emotions acceptably. Most children are told how *not* to express emotions. Few are taught the flip side of the same coin—how to express the emotions in socially acceptable ways.

Another area for children to learn about is their own rights. Children have rights, as do all human beings. For years in the past, women and children were considered chattel. They had fewer rights than cattle. The history of children can be read in many books about child development so I will not dwell on the unpleasantness considered acceptable for "owners" to foist on children. Just as women and minority groups have been able to attain rights legally, so we are moving toward the day when children will receive legal protection in the fullest sense. This does not mean the right to stay up late or talk back or other fears that some people often interpret as children's rights. Children should have the right not to be abused, not to be considered liars with the burden of proof on their shoulders in legal situations with adults, and the right to say NO to adults when they feel threatened or uncomfortable. They should have the right to be believed and the right to be respected as children and not treated as chattel or miniature adults. What we should tell children and how we should talk to them about their rights are topics covered further in this chapter.

CURRICULUM CONTENT

Family

Children are born part of a family. They grow up in a family. Family is the basic unit of human existence. What is family? *Family* is as diverse a word today as is *love* or *reality.* When you work with children on self-concept development, the place to begin is with family. Talk to the children about what they think a family is. The answers vary, but they usually include a place to live and sleep, a place where you get hugs and love, the people I live with who care about me, mommy and daddy, and so on. Family is the unit in which you live with caring people. Families can be small or big, have children or not, have grandparents or other adults or not; but all have love.

To help children visualize *family,* you can display posters or magazine pictures of single parents with children, two parents with children, two adults without children, and various versions of extended families. The children can talk about families and cut out from magazines "their" family—one mom, two dads, or whatever fits their family picture. Talk about how families help each other and how the children themselves contribute to the family.

Each Child as Individual

From the family discussion, next begin talking about the individual child as a unique and special person. The children already know that they are each part of a family, and they are ready to learn more about each other. The first thing to talk about is name. They have been singing and playing name games to get to know each other. Now, they can ask each other, "What do you like about your name?, Do you know what your name means?, How did you get your special name? Have the children spell their names in glitter or macaroni.

The next step is learning about *me.* You can make me books and me puppets. A me book has one page for the child's self-portrait, address, and a picture of where he or she lives, telephone number, and then many other pages about favorite colors, foods, animals, and so on. Each page can be drawn or pasted or be in three-dimensional form, at the child's discretion. For example, for the color page, the children can draw a picture in their favorite color, or paint, or make a colored sand picture on glue, or iron crayon shavings between wax paper and mount it, or paste a design. The books should be fun and should let the children see how individual and special each one can be. Simultaneously, the children make three-dimensional houses out of shoeboxes or milk cartons and eventually have a whole town. Another project to make is puppets that require the children to look at themselves in the mirror for detail. What color eyes do you need for your puppet? What color yarn for your hair? These are just some questions they need to answer. Puppets can be made out of paper lunch bags; or a popsickle or craft stick with a circle face stapled to it; or a toilet-paper roll with arms, legs, and face attached; for example. You can also trace and color the children's whole bodies on large sheets of paper. Discussion while working on these projects helps foster a sense of who I am and where I belong.

The Body

Using games and fingerplays is helpful in learning body parts and how they work. For the young child, these body name and function discoveries are usually great fun and keep their interest. It is fascinating to find out that you have ankles and that they can wiggle around, and that without them you would walk like a stiff soldier. Acting out and exercising the parts also helps us to learn about our fantastic body machines. Even young children should be taught the correct names for the body parts. Often, some of the longest and most difficult names are the ones children remembered best. Learning the correct names eliminates confusion and misunderstandings. For example, what do you call the part on which you sit? *Tush? Bum? Behind?* Or do you have another cute name? *Gluteus maximus* is the name of the big muscle that comprises the bum. The children love it. There is no mixup on what part of the body they are speaking about. The youngest child can usually remember every jingle on television, so if the body parts are learned through song even two-year-olds can learn and remember the names of their body parts.

It also is important for children to learn the names of the sexual parts of the body. Casually and in a nonemphasizing manner, children should be taught that boys and men have a penis and girls and women have a vulva. This should be said in positive terms and not in a manner that makes little ones feel they are missing a part. Cute terms are dangerous for children. A common-sense approach to learning all body part names should be implemented from the first time your child asks, "What is this part?" No part of the child is bad. Ignoring a part or avoiding it usually heightens interest. Also, the children do not have to unlearn names about which other children might tease them as baby names.

Once the children have worked on me books, send the books home and encourage the children to read and reread the book with family and friends. It is interesting to find that people do not always know what children think is special about themselves. The reading also opens up other conversation and communication between parent and child.

Emotions

Once the children have practiced and learned their body names, they are ready to delve into the discussion and study of emotions. This has been a much neglected area of children's learning. The easiest way to start is with the emotion of feeling *happy*. First, talk about what is happy, what makes you happy, and how it feels to be happy. Allow enough time for all children to participate. After everyone has a turn, ask once more for the things that make most of us feel happy and write them on a large piece of paper. Whether or not the children can read, this is an important step. You are validating their feelings by writing them down. This proves how important the children's input is. One warning—let each child speak even if all remarks are not relevant. Positively reinforce each child's contribution and then use your written conclusion to emphasize points that you feel best relate.

After this discussion, ask the children to play a role play game. Cite some examples of situations and they tell if the situation would make them happy or not happy.

Examples

Dad gave me a big hug today.

I was hurt and Mom came and helped me feel better with a bandage and a cookie.

Jenny took my favorite toy and won't give it back.

Then ask the children to give some examples or to act out a few situations.

The next day, go through the same process with the other side of happy or what do I do that makes other people happy. Immediately following the emotion *happy* is *sad.* Follow the same process as for happy, but now in the role play and examples the children can say whether it is a happy or a sad feeling for them. When the two sad days are over, have the children make a paper plate face and add a half moon mouth that is attached with a brad fastener so the mouth can move from happy to sad to relate to the review story situations.

The next emotions covered are surprise and fear. These emotions are close in how we react to them. The same process is followed, except for that role

Children enjoy dramatizing their emotions. Using stories and allowing children to act them out is a terrific reinforcement.

play also serves as a review of happy and sad while the children practice surprise. During the role plays, ask the children to show the face that goes with each emotion. The last emotion covered with younger children is anger (with older children, one can get more involved with secondary emotions: frustration, pride, for example). Anger is one of the most difficult emotions for human beings to handle, and more so for children. Since children do not have our adult verbal skills and are more apt to react in a physical manner to anger, it is important to work on positive ways to handle anger. Notice that this does not say "ways to negate anger." Anger is as valid an emotion as any other. Feelings are not black or white, right or wrong. Feelings are—period. Many adults *say* they do not get angry, but they do. It is important to validate the emotion and then to handle it in a socially acceptable manner. After the same process is followed for the first two days of discussion, change the role plays to inquisitive discussions on how the child should handle the following situation.

Examples

Sally comes out from snack and finds her little brother next to her broken new miniwheel. What would you do if you were Sally? (Initially, answers include *kill, bite, wham him,* etc.—very physical and instant reactions.) After these answers, change the situation to add: Sally's little brother did not break the miniwheel. Joey did and then he ran home. Now ask the children: How do you think Sally feels after she hit her brother and he didn't even do it? After this discussion, ask the children what Sally could have done *before* she acted with the hitting. Then introduce the phrase, "I am so angry when . . . (in this case, when you break my miniwheel)!" The phrase can be yelled or spoken angrily; the main idea is to give the angry child a quick *verbal* vent for the anger while giving the other party a chance to explain before it comes to physical action. What you are doing is implanting the idea of options and rights to children on a level to which they can relate. In Sally's case, she now is not guilty or defensive because she hit her brother. She handled her anger. Her brother got to tell the story as it happened and not as Sally assumed from appearances. Sally did not violate her brother's right not to be hit. Further discussions could include how would you feel if you were accused and hit for something you did not do. This discussion reinforces the option of feeling for the other person.

In the classroom, allow any child to use the phrase "I am so angry when . . ." to express anger. Many parents may tell of the positive carry over at home. At least, you know the child is upset and over what. Using this phrase also gives you a few seconds to intercede if it appears fists will follow. It is difficult to be a child and learn to share your world with others. It is important that children learn that anger does not give them the right to take away another person's right to safety.

Anger is the most difficult emotion for most children. They are always told how not to express it and rarely told how to express it in socially acceptable ways.

What if there is no apparent reason for anger or a child is going to burst with anger and needs an outlet? A great deal of controversy exists about whether expressing anger feeds or lessens it. There are ways an adult can safely allow a child to blow off steam that involve no harm to others, such as with a punching bag in the classroom, complete with gloves. If a child cannot contain anger, that anger can be dispensed safely rather than taken out physically on others. A boxing bag requires good eye-hand coordination and quickly tires the child. Class rules can demand that the child put on the gloves first, stand with two feet on the marked spot, and then box. With disturbed or very acting-out children, allow them to use the punching bag as needed. Another helpful venting solution is to allow an acting-out child to punch pillows while verbally expressing anger. This practice changes negative energy into positive because it also cleans the pillows! Of course, the idea is to redirect physical aggression into more verbal and socially acceptable forms of expression. As a temporary intermediary step, for some children should be allowed to get out the physical expression while learning new verbal techniques. Allowing a physical release does not increase the physical release tendencies. You should also follow up expressions of anger with discussions on how the child handled it and what could have been done differently. The follow up is important to helping change the behavioral expression. Of course, the child's right to the feeling of anger is never negated. The child should never be allowed to harm other children or property or the teacher. People and their property are not free expression items.

Personal Space

This is a good time to introduce the concept of *personal invisible space.* Every person has an invisible space around that person that is his or hers alone. You may chose to let people into this circle, but you may not want others there. You have the right to deny others access into your personal space, and they the right to deny access to you. Hitting someone violates that person's personal space. This concept is easily proven to children. Clap your arms in front and in back. That is most people's space area. To prove the idea, have a close friend walk up close and hug you. Now have a stranger walk up and do the same. There was probably a point at which you felt uncomfortable. That point is the beginning of your own invisible personal space. Tell the children that this space is like Spiderman's spider sense—invisible but important. Adults often negate children's rights to privacy to the point at which children sometimes lose their natural reaction to adults who violate their personal space.

Examples

Ms. Jones the teacher, likes to ruffle children's hair as a sign of favor.

Sammy is told he has to kiss Uncle Hank even after he expressed to his parents a desire not to.

Frannie's parents ignore her yelling when their family friend keeps tickling her when she's yelled NO.

These people have violated the child's right to personal space and are sending the child a message that the child has to do what the bigger and stronger adults say or want regardless of the child's feelings or desires.

None of these examples are bad if the child is enjoying the attention and does not feel upset by it. However, a child who feels uncomfortable or troubled by the attention should be respected for this feeling and not forced. The teacher can respond by not ruffling John's hair and giving verbal praise; Sammy's parents can substitute a handshake by telling Uncle Hank that Sammy wants to say hello with a handshake; and Frannie's parents could intervene with a few well

Positive self-concept is very important to foster as a prerequisite for safety training. Making likenesses is a fun way for children to increase their positive feelings about themselves.

chosen words. Such situations do not have to become major problems, but neither should a child be taught or forced to ignore personal feelings to satisfy other people. It need not be impolite or rude to allow the child personal space. A child who knows he or she has the right to tune into individual feelings about personal space, who knows the parents will be supportive, and who knows he or she can say NO if someone intrudes on the right to personal space is a safer, more secure child. Such a child is much less apt to be victimized. This concept is built on more fully in chapter 6. It is enough now that the idea has been planted with the child.

By this point, the child should have strengthened self-concept enough that safety training can begin. The next four chapters deal with the four building block steps to safety for the child.

FIGURE 2.1
Let the children cut out or draw for themselves people they feel belong here. You can label the pictures for children who are too young to write.

WORDS AND PHRASES THAT HELP BUILD POSITIVE SELF-CONCEPTS

wonderful
awesome
super
fabulous
good try
terrific
neat
perfect
great
outstanding
fantastic
excellent
marvelous
brilliant
thank you

That's clever!
That was a good choice!
Keep trying, great going!
I'm most proud of the way you . . .
You're doing better!
What great imagination!
You catch on fast!
I like the way you . . .
You are doing so well!
That shows good thought!
How interesting!
Now you're cooking . . . !
That shows a lot of work on your part!

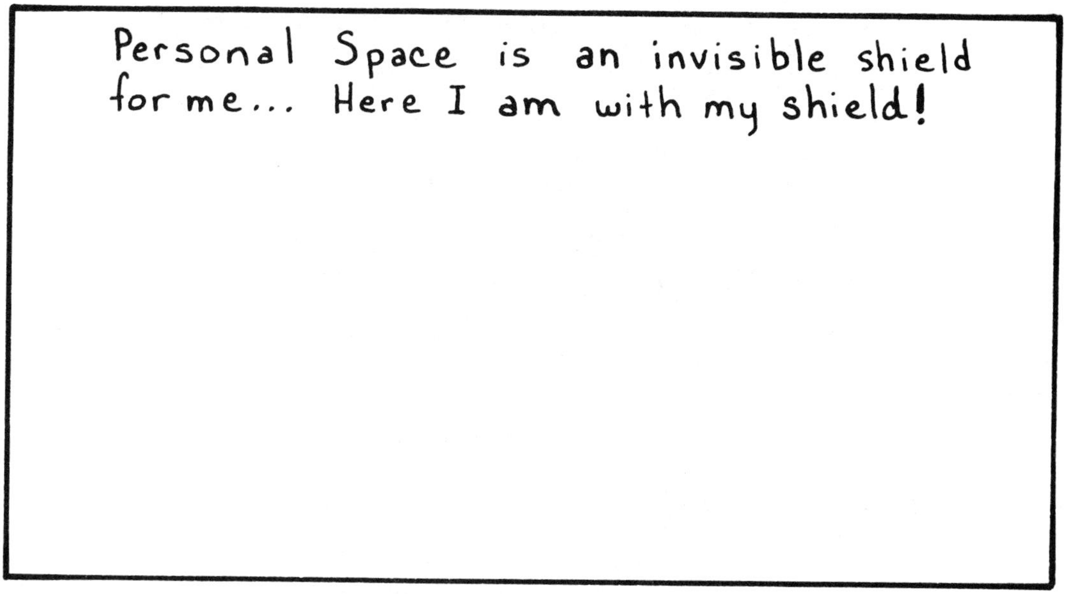

Personal Space is an invisible shield for me... Here I am with my shield!

FIGURE 2.2
Here, the children can draw their own pictures with how they see the invisible space. Another possibility is to have the children draw just themselves and then cover each picture with clear plastic wrap or a plastic bag.

Your cooperation really helped!
Great effort!
Way to go!
Everyone makes mistakes, try again!
I make mistakes too! That's how we learn!
Thank you for helping!
I'm proud of you!
That's supercalifragilisticexpealidotious!
Keep it up, you're almost there!

splendid
fine job
top job
boss
all right

Also use your body language to reinforce the positive: A hand shake, a pat on the back, or a clap whatever the child feels confortable with. Joking also can be a positive reinforcement between a child and an adult.

QUESTIONS FOR REVIEW

1. What is a self-concept?
2. What are some common stereotypes about young children?
3. How should you praise a child?
4. How does talking and sharing feelings help develop self-concept in a positive manner?
5. Is it true that children have no need to learn social skills?
6. We tell children how not to express themselves but we forget to tell them ______________________________ ______________________________ ______________________________.
7. What kind of rights are we talking about when we speak of children's rights?
8. What is a family?
9. What is a me book? Why and how would you make one?
10. Can you name three ways to replicate yourself to help foster self-concepts and learning?
11. Should children at a young age be taught correct anatomical names for body parts?
12. How can they be taught such difficult terms?
13. Do you teach sexual terms to the young child? What names should be used?
14. Why teach emotional health to young children?
15. How can you teach an emotion to a young child?
16. What phrase can be used in lieu of a physical reaction to anger?
17. What is the controversy about anger and expression with young children?
18. What is personal space?

CHAPTER 3

First Aid and My Teddy Bear

BASIC FIRST AID

Basic first aid can be one of the most important subjects you will teach children. It dovetails well with what children learn in their early life. Young children are learning about their bodies and how they work. It is normal for young children to be overly concerned about "boo-boos" and injuries. It is normal for preschoolers especially to carry on over minor injuries because they do not always have a clear idea that they are, in fact, all right. The body is tougher than children realize. On the other hand, children must learn that the body is not indestructible.

Young children experience various stages and types of fear as they grow. One fear is that something might happen to a parent or caregiver. Between the ages of two and five, the physical fears begin to give way as the children learn about their bodies and as they learn what they can and cannot do with their bodies. "During the same age span, there was an increase in fear of imaginary creatures . . . and threat of harm (for example, from traffic, deep water, fire or other potentially dangerous situations). The latter fears develop as children gain greater awareness of things and become capable of anticipating potential danger."[1]

1. Robert F. Biehler, *Child Development: An Introduction,* Second Edition, p. 353. Copyright © 1981 by Houghton Mifflin Company. Used by permission.

Three methods can help children become less fearful and more competent.

- *Explaining the situation.* The child who is afraid will be less frightened when he/she is told what to expect, why something happens, and what to do about it or how to handle it.
- *Setting an example.* The child who sees the adult handle situations well will respond better himself/herself in the situation. Children also benefit from seeing their peers respond well to a given situation. Children often will try something because someone their own size did it.
- *Positive reconditioning.* Exposing the child to a situation in a safe manner where he/she can come to terms with it at their own readiness goes a long way in helping him/her overcome a fear.
- *Helping the child gain confidence in dealing with the feared object or situation.* The most effective way to help a child overcome a fear is to teach him or her to become competent in dealing with it.[2]

Basic first aid training accomplishes these goals through the methods recommended to eliminate fear. The American Red Cross offers standard first aid for all people in the United States. The cost is minimal, and the knowledge is invaluable. Every parent and every person who works with children should take the training. Many people take incorrect action in an emergency because they lack current training. Many procedures that were correct ten or fifteen years ago have been found to be detrimental to the victim and thus have been changed.

The first thing young children should be taught is their address and telephone number. In any emergency, a child might have to call for help. The police, ambulance, and emergency people cannot get to the child or the situation if the child cannot relay the information. If the child is hurt and alone, no one can contact the appropriate adult if the child does not know where he or she belongs.

Learning their telephone number and address should be fun for children. The importance can be stressed, but the child will learn better through songs or jingles than through a formal learning situation. We know how easily children remember commercials.

Here is one example of a good song to learn your name:

Example

"HERE I AM   sung to: 'Where is Thumbkin?'

Where is __________?   *adult's part*

Where is __________?

2. Biehler, 353–355. Used by permission.

Here I am!	(child stands up)	*child's part*
Here I am!		
How are you today, sir/madam?		*adult's part*
Very well, thank you		*child's part*
Please sit down.		*both can sing*
Please sit down."[3]		

Many song books and records contain songs that relate to learning body parts, names, addresses, telephone numbers, and safety. One of the easiest books series for people with no formal music or teaching expertise is *Piggyback Songs* compiled by Jean Warren and published by Totline Press. The lyrics are all sung to familiar tunes so they are easy to use.

Learning addresses can be fun if the children make replicas of their houses out of a box or a container. While coloring and pasting on windows, the children can be repeating their address. Try playing a game in which you are the police or fire fighter who has to get to a child's home. Everytime the child gives the correct address, the police can get to the house and save it. A piece of cardboard with a house and a road makes a fine game board. A toy car can serve as the police or fire vehicle.

Telephone skills are also important and again fun to learn. A toy telephone and role plays can help. Using a telephone song is a fun way for children to learn numbers. Have your child call you from a neighbor's or friend's house. This is good practice. Learning the emergency number for your town is also valuable. Very young children can learn to dial zero.

When the children have learned who they are and where they live, they are ready to learn first aid. "Ask what is it that each of you is going to have to do before you can help anyone in any type of emergency. This is the first rule in BAT [Basic Aid Training] class."[4] The answer is *stay calm*. If you are calm, you will remember what to do and how to help a victim. Have young children count to three so they will be forced to get calm by concentrating on counting. The next step is to do the first aid they know or to get help. The final step is to stay with the person, speaking calmly until help comes. This last step is important with young children, especially if an adult is hurt. Speaking calmly will help calm the child and staying there will keep the child from running in panic and possibly getting hurt.

Children should learn how to telephone for help. Using the phone and role playing are the most helpful ways to learn this skill. When calling, the child

3. Song by Gail Ray of Fort Worth, Texas. From *Piggyback Songs*, compiled by Jean Warren (Everett, Wash.: Totline Press, Warren Publishing House, Inc., 1983), 53. Used by permission.

4. American National Red Cross, *Basic Aid Training* (Washington, D.C.: ARC, 1980), 7.

needs to give the four *W*'s; *who* is calling, *where* you are calling from, *what* happened (Mommy fell down; Susie won't talk, she's all white), and *wait* for the person on the telephone to tell you what to do then *wait* with the person. It is very important that the child learn to wait on the telephone! The operator might need more information; the child might need to be reminded to open a door so when help arrives they can get into the house. Practice this over and over. It is also helpful for children to feel they can do something if an adult were hurt. It is also comforting to know there is someone the children can reach to help them and tell them what to do if they forget.

The basic first aid procedures recommended to teach young children are treatments for cuts, bumps, nosebleeds, burns, fainting, a fall, bug bites, and poison. The knowledge you expect them to have is very basic. Can they tell if the injury is minor, like a tiny scratch they can wash and bandage, or is it a big cut that needs treatment? Expect the child to be able to get help. Talk

Learning first aid procedures on a basic level is easy and fun for young children. Teddy bears make terrific models for play and practice.

about why you would follow the recommended steps and how the child can tell what needs to be done. Try to get the child to tell why the steps should be done.

Have the children practice first aid on a doll or a teddy bear. Practicing on Teddy is fun and saves on real people wear-and-tear that overenthusiastic children are apt to give.

Change the situation somewhat each time it is practiced so the children learn to discriminate and see the situation through the changes. After the children have learned the first aid in the book, have them take the book home and read it with their parents. Give a test on the learnings. Have someone other than the trainer test each child with his or her doll or teddy bear.

Example

For example, the tester can say:
"Teddy went out in the yard. He saw the honey and tried to get it. Oh, no! The bees saw him! The bee stung poor Teddy on his nose. What can you do to help Teddy?"

See if the child can perform the correct first aid. At the end of the test, sign the certificate of First Aid and present it to the child with a bit of fanfare for a job well done! To help with lesson reinforcement, follow up with making the first aid kit in Figure 3.1 and let the children play with dolls and Teddy. On their own, children like to play first aid.

Adults periodically need to ask the children what they would do if . . . . No child and few adults can remember without refreshers all of the first aid procedures. Another good refresher is to let the children help handle emergencies when they happen, especially the minor ones that seem to occur so often. Such activities as getting the ice and wrapping it in a towel can help children become aware of their competence. You can also add new first aid procedures as you feel the children are ready for them, or add specialized medical situations.

Example

Daddy has asthma and this is what we do if Daddy starts to wheeze or look funny.

Children can handle situations if taught ahead of time what to do and allowed to think through why they should act a certain way in a given situation.

The First Aid Handbook illustrated in Figure 3.2 is a book to create with the children. Each section can be a separate page.

When teaching first aid procedures, remember to have the children practice naming body parts. This is important. Use jingles and songs to help them remember. Two good songs for body parts reinforcement are "If You're Happy and You Know It" and "Head and Shoulders." These songs can be found in almost any music book.

First Aid Kit for Very Young Children

vinyl wallpaper sheet } usually available for free (discount wallpaper store books)

1. double except for flap
2. punch holes on sides
3. let children string (sew) with yarn
4. print name on flap

Place inside: cotton balls, cotton swabs
bandages
prepackaged wet ones or wipes
gauze pads
adhesive tape
paper and pencil

First Aid Kit is to be used to practice on Teddy bears or dolls! Never practice on baby sisters or brothers.

Additional fun equipment: empty, clean (nonresistant cap) bottle*
needleless syringes
tongue depressors
(for medical playacting)

Other kit ideas:

shoebox

covered cereal box (oaktag strap)

Hats: cardboard or oaktag band. Staple on butter tin for a medical look.

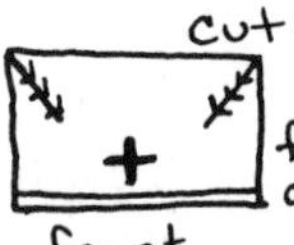

* cheerios make fine pretend medication

FIGURE 3.1
Suggestions for making a first aid kit.

FIGURE 3.2
Sample first aid book to make with children.

Cuts, Scrapes

1. Hold cut up. (gravity helps)
2. Press on cut. (direct pressure)
3. Wash cut, put on bandage.
4. If it keeps bleeding, get help!

Bumps, Bruises

1. Get ice and/or a cold wet towel.
2. Place it on the bump.
3. If person is dizzy, have him or her lie down.
4. Get help!

Nosebleeds

1. Keep head in regular position.
2. Pinch hard at the nostrils.
3. Hold tissue under nose.
4. Clean up if after five minutes the nose is fine.
5. If still bleeding, get help.

DO NOT BLOW NOSE!

Burns

<u>Small burn</u> - red

1. Put cold water, ice or snow on burn.

<u>Middle-size burn</u> - blister

1. Put cool water, not ice, on burn.
2. Get help!
   DO NOT BREAK BLISTERS.

<u>Worst burn</u> - burnt skin

1. Cover with clean cloth; use a dry cloth.
   DO NOT USE WATER!
2. Get help - FAST!

Sample first aid book.

Fainting

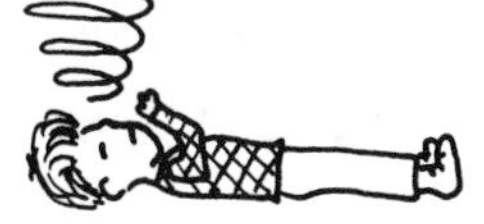

Person has pale, cool skin; can be sweaty or dizzy.

1. Have person lie down

2. Loosen shirt

3. Get help!

Falls

1. Leave person there- do not move him or her.

2. Get help!

Bug bites

<u>Mosquito</u> - wash bite, do not scratch - baking soda helps!

<u>Bee</u> - put on baking soda or mud - remove stinger with tweezers. If person swells - get help!

<u>Tick</u> - GET AN ADULT! pour cooking oil over bug - then remove bug with tweezers.

Do not use matches, gasoline or alcohol!

Poisons

1. See if you can find what the person ate or smelled

2. Get help!

Call Poison Center!

Sample first aid book.

In an Emergency!

Junior First Aiders:

1. Remain calm! Count to three and think!

2. Do the first aid and/or get help!
3. Wait with the person until help comes!
4. Talk softly and calmly with the person!

When you call for help:

The four W's!

WHO, WHAT, WHERE, WAIT.

1. give your name.
2. tell where you are.
3. tell what happened.
4. speak calmly and wait at the phone until the operator tells you what to do.

Sample first aid book.

Post me near the telephone.

my name is ______________

I live at ______________

my telephone number is ______________

fire ______________ police ______________

poison ______________ ambulance ______________

MOM ______________ DAD ______________

telephone friend ______________ telephone friend ______________

Doctor ______________ Doctor ______________

my doctor my doctor

Remember Your Telephone Safety!

Be a telephone Detective!

1. Never tell your name.
2. Never tell if parent is <u>not</u> home.
3. If you are nervous—HANG UP!

You do not have to answer the telephone's questions!

Sample first aid book.

Bring in a skeleton and let the children learn that they have bones inside that help them stand and move. Let them act out as skeletons and then pretend they have no skeleton. What happens? Also, muscles and how they work are fascinating to young children. A simple yet accurate explanation for young children is to say that muscles are like elastics that stretch and move the bones so you can move.

Don't forget to have the junior first aider keep practicing telephone skills, too. Put a toy telephone in the pretend ambulance or hospital.

Dressing up, making medical kits, having a nurse or doctor visit the classroom, and setting up a pretend hospital at home or in the classroom are great follow-ups to this unit. You can also visit a local hospital. Most hospitals are delighted to have young children tour. Such tours can eliminate fears in children who have been there only for frightening emergencies or unpleasant

Making first aid kits is a great follow-up activity to learning first aid. Cereal put into non-safety-top bottles makes wonderful Teddy medicine.

testing. A visit to the hospital switchboard usually can be included on your hospital tour if you ask ahead.

Hahnemann Hospital in Worcester, Massachusetts sets up the trip with a wonderful introduction. The children are dressed as hospital personnel; first, a "sick" child is brought in, and then a child who fell. The children dramatize the scene with directions from the volunteers. Then they play a "Guess-Which-Part" game using X-rays. The children love these activities. The tour follows throughout the entire hospital and ends with juice and cookies and certificates for all. The hospital trip is best taken in the fall, after completing the first aid and Teddy bear chapter.

One note about making first aid kits—use only sterile syringes *without* needles for health safety reasons. You can obtain clean and sterile materials from local drug stores and medical supply houses. Use non-safety-cap bottles and fill with nutritious snacks rather than with sugar cereals. This is a good time to remind children *never* to take medications on their own.

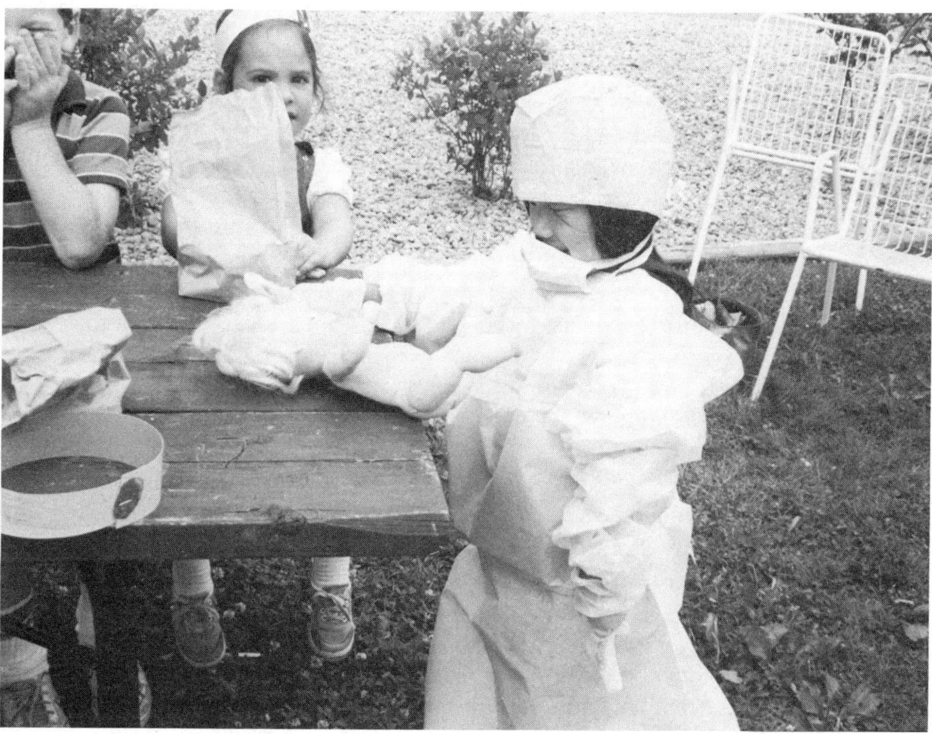

Hospitals are wonderful resources. Disposable surgical clothing can turn first aid practice into a realistic situation. Hospital tours also provide the opportunity for realistic role play.

DENTAL CONCERNS AND NUTRITION

Material on dental care is included in this chapter on first aid because learning competency about the body and its immediate workings is a strong primary building block to set up a strong self-concept on which we can build later. Young children are fascinated by their teeth.

Have toothbrushes for each child in your program, and have all children brush after snacks. Make this a priority. Borrow a large set of teeth from a local dentist. Use these to initiate discussions about what teeth are and why we have them. Colgate Company has some excellent filmstrips and hand-out materials available at minimal cost or for no cost. These filmstrips use "Happy Tooth" (a tooth character who tells children about good care of teeth) and such cartoon characters as Nancy and Sluggo. Even two-year-olds can learn that teeth have parts; that some teeth have the job of cutting food and others have the jobs of grinding, tearing, and chewing; and that teeth have friends and enemies.

We learn that the friends are the dentist, hygienist, toothbrush, toothpaste, and good foods. It is important for children to learn about these good friends at an early age so they do not fear dentists, especially if a first visit is for decay treatment. Most pediatric dentists recommend that children visit for cleanings around the age of two. This early visit helps children develop positive feeling about the dentist and dental care. Some dentists give children a toothbrush as a teething tool when they are breaking in two-year molars. It helps. Children should use soft toothbrushes. A hard or medium brush rips their gums. Younger children can be taught flossing by using disposable flossers. These flossers are small and have a handle just right for little hands. Using this implement eliminates the aggravation of wrapping floss and then trying to fit little hands into the child's own mouth. The children can also do it themselves. Dr. Bruce S. Fieldman, a pediatric dentist who strongly advocates preventative dentistry with children, recommends allowing children to floss after brushing while watching television or sitting in another room. The children will do a more thorough job and you do not have to stand over them in the bathroom. Dr. Fieldman also advocates limiting sugary sweets for young children, who are not the best brushers. If they have an occasional sweet, the children should brush immediately after. Most damage is done to the tooth within the first ten or fifteen minutes after eating.

Sealents are another new tool in the prevention of dental cavities. Check them out for your own children and talk to parents about them if you are a teacher. Even children with hereditary so-called soft teeth can cut back on cavities with this new technique. Consult with local dentists. You will find some who are great resources.

Once the children have learned about teeth, talk about the enemies of good teeth. We can fight these enemies, and the children can help. In fact, the children are the leaders in the fight.

Mr. Tooth Decay is an ugly old meanie who keeps tooth decay monsters to dig holes in uncared-for teeth. Make up plays and stories about him. The children love acting out these skits, especially when the good guys chase away the monsters. Make toothbrushes out of spaghetti and happy tooth out of white playdough and have many follow-up art activities. While doing these activities, the children are learning that candy, baked goods, and highly sugared treats make the monsters happy and can cause teeth to be holey and very unhappy.

Also start a massive Antisugar campaign. Correlate it with a regular cooking and nutrition program—Chef Combo from the New England Dairy Council is a terrific kit with cooking and nutrition ideas available at minimal cost and free workshops for teachers. Check with your local Dairy Council.

Have the children watch the television ads for cereals. After a few days, talk about the ads. The lobby to push nonnutritious foods on children is strong. Television commercials use cartoon characters and music and colors that have been researched to entice children. The ads also always say the cereal is part of a nutritious breakfast. They are not really lying because the breakfast is shown with juice, toast, and milk. What they do not tell the child is that the cereal is 50 percent or more sugar and other nonnutritious fillers. The result of the ads is visible in any grocery store cereal aisle. When talking about the ads, encourage the children to become discretionary in their thinking. Tell the children that the ad lies and was made tricky on purpose. After discussing one ad, talk about others; the children soon become very adept at criticizing the ads. They like the cartoon characters, but with little direct intervention, the children conclude that they are smarter than the ad makers. Then switch strategy and talk about which cereals are good for them and have a tasting party to try them. Add cinnamon or fruits to see if the tastes are better.

A list of cereals and their sugar content is given in Figure 3.3. This list can be sent home to parents. The less sugar, the better for the child. Note how many frequently advertised cereals are 40 or 50 percent sugar.

Then discuss snacks in a similar manner. Which snacks are high in sugar or fillers? Why don't we want to eat them all the time? Are there snacks that fight decay and are good for our bodies? Can you name some? We use our cooking time to make some easy and fun to eat snacks that are nutritious. Instead of advocating to the parents to provide good and nutritious snacks, make this the children's responsibility.

It may appear that the past few pages have not focused on safety, but think about what was covered. The children have learned that not everything is good for them. They have learned they can do certain self-care activities by themselves. The children have learned that not all things they see or are told are true or are good for them even if an adult or television tells them so. We have planted the seed of the idea that the children should listen carefully and with discrimination to what they are told. This seed will bear fruit later. The children also have gained a sense of control over some of the things about themselves.

Finding Sugar in Your Packaged Food Purchases

1. Look for the Nutritional Information Per Serving side of the package.
2. Check for the Carbohydrate listing per serving. It is usually listed in grams.
3. Most packages contain carbohydrate information at the bottom that breaks down the carbohydrates into their component parts of starches, sucroses and sugars, and fillers. This is where you can judge the real sugar content of the serving.
4. Check the ingredient listing when there is no carbohydrate information listing or if you are in doubt about the sugar level. The ingredients are listed by their amounts in decreasing order. In order words, the first listed makes up the largest percentage of the ingredients used to make the product.
5. Be aware of alternative names for sugar such as sucrose, honey, fructose, corn syrup, brown sugar, and corn syrup solids. Even if sugar is not listed as a first or second ingredient, you may find two or three different sugar names given in various places in the list of ingredients. This means that the sugar content is high despite sugar not being at the top of the list.
6. One ounce is equal to 28.35 grams (g). One ounce is a fairly standard serving size, although some boxes will list a serving of fewer grams.

   Sample: 1 serving (1 oz.) = 28.35 g of brand X cereal
   carbohydrates = 24 g
   sucrose and other sugars = 12 g

   In this cereal 12 grams of the 28.35 grams per serving are sugar. The sugar content is almost one-half of the serving—obviously a high sugar content cereal.

Common Cereals and Their Sugar Content

Cereal Company	*Name of Cereal*	*Serving Size (28.35 g = 1 oz.)*	*Grams of Sugar per Serving*
General Mills	Cheerios	1¼ cup	1
	Cocoa Puffs	1 cup	11
	Honey Nut Cheerios	¾ cup	10
	Kix	1½ cup	3
	Lucky Charms	1 cup	11
	Total	1 cup	3
Kellogg's	Apple Jacks	1 cup	14
	Corn Flakes	1 cup	2
	Corn Pops	1 cup	12
	Fruit Loops	1 cup	13
	Frosted Flakes	1 cup	11
	Honey Smacks	¾ cup	15
	OJ'S	1 cup	11
	Raisin Bran	¾ cup with raisins	10
	Rice Krispies	1 cup	3
	Frosted Rice Krispies	1 cup	11

***FIGURE* 3.3**
Dental facts.

Cereal Company	*Name of Cereal*	*Serving Size (28.35 g = 1 oz.)*	*Grams of Sugar per Serving*
Nabisco	Shredded Wheat	⅔ cup	0
	Team Flakes	1 cup	5
Post	Alpha-Bits	1 cup	11
	Cocoa Pebbles	⅞ cup	13
	Fruit & Fiber (Tropical)	½ cup	6
	Fruit & Fiber (Date, etc.)	½ cup	7
	Fruity Pebbles	⅞ cup	12
	Honey Comb	1⅓ cup	11
Quaker	Cap'n Crunch	¾ cup	12
	Life	⅔ cup	6
	Oatmeal (Old Fashioned)	⅓ cup	only listed total
	Oh's Honey Graham	1 cup	11
	100% Natural Cereal	¼ cup	5
	Puffed Rice	1 cup	0
	Puffed Wheat	1 cup	0
Ralston	Bran Chex	⅔ cup	5
	Corn Chex	1 cup	3
	Rice Chex	1⅛ cup	2
	Wheat Chex	⅔ cup	2
	Ghost Buster	1 cup	not listed
Uhlmann	Old Fashion Maltex	1 cup	1
Maypo	Maypo (Vermont Style)	¼ cup	3

Some general guidelines:

1. Less is best—fewer ingredients.
2. Plainer foods contain less sugar.
3. The more convenient, the less nutritious are hot cereals.
4. Dried fruits add to the sugar content when included in the cereal.
5. Beware of toaster pop and granola bar easy breakfasts—they are usually high in sugar.
6. The more dramatic and pushy the television commercial, generally the less nutritious is the cereal. Several companies try to sell sugary cereals with clever, child-researched methods. Tell children that the cereal is a rip-off. Let children help you check boxes and find a cereal that is good to eat and low in sugar.

Hidden Sugars in Foods

The parent often says, "Doctor, my children don't eat sugar!" Here are the approximate amounts of refined sugar hidden in common foods—about which the parent is usually unaware.

Beverages	*Serving Size*	*Teaspoons of Sugar per Serving*
Cola drinks	1 6 oz. glass	4½
Ginger Ale	1 6 oz. glass	3½
Orange Ade	1 8 oz. glass	5
Root Beer	1 10 oz. glass	4½
Seven-Up	1 6 oz. glass	4½
Soda pop	1 8 oz. glass	5
Sweet cider	1 cup	4½
Jams and Jellies		
Apple butter	1 tbsp.	1
Jelly	1 tbsp.	4–6
Orange marm.	1 tbsp.	4–6
Peach butter	1 tbsp.	1
Strawberry jam	1 tbsp.	4
Candies		
Candy bar	1	2½
Chewing gum	1 stick	½
Chocolate cream	1 piece	2
Fudge	1 inch cube	4½
Gumdrop	1	2
Hard candy	4 oz.	20
Lifesavers	1	½
Peanut brittle	1 oz.	3½
Marshmallow	1	1½
Fruits and Canned Juices		
Raisins	½ cup	4
Currants, dried	1 tbsp.	4
Prunes, dried	3–4 med.	4
Apricots, dried	4–6 halves	4
Dates, dried	3–4	4½
Figs, dried	2 small	4½
Fruit cocktail	½ cup	5
Rhubarb, stewed	½ cup	8
Applesauce	½ cup	2
Canned peaches	2 halves and 1 T. syrup	3½
Orange juice	½ cup	2
Pineapple juice unsweetened	½ cup	2½
Grape juice	½ cup	3½
Canned fruit juice	½ cup	2

Bread and Cereals	*Serving Size*	*Teaspoons of Sugar per Serving*
White bread	1 slice	½
Corn Flakes, Wheaties, etc.	1 bowl and 1 T. sugar	4–8
Hamburger bun	1	3
Hot dog bun	1	3
Cakes and Cookies		
Angel food cake	1 4 oz. piece	7
Applesauce cake	1 4 oz. piece	5½
Banana cake	1 2 oz. piece	2
Cheese cake	1 4 oz. piece	2
Chocolate cake	1 4 oz. piece	8
Coffee cake	1 4 oz. piece	4½
Cupcake—iced	1	6
Jelly roll	1 2 oz. piece	2½
Pound cake	1 4 oz. piece	5
Brownies	1 small	3
Molasses cookie	1	2
Chocolate cookie	1	1½
Fig Newton	1	5
Ginger snap	1	3
Macaroon	1	6
Oatmeal cookie	1	2
Sugar cookie	1	1½
Cream puff	1	2
Donut, plain	1	3
Donut, iced	1	6
Dairy Products		
Ice cream	3½ oz.	3½
Ice cream bar	1	5
Ice cream cone	1	3½
Ice cream soda	1	5
Cocoa, all milk	1 cup	4
Ice cream sundae	1	7
Chocolate milk	1 5 oz. cup	6
Sherbert	½ cup	9
Desserts		
Apple cobbler	½ cup	3
Custard	½ cup	2
Jello	½ cup	4½
Apple pie	1 aver. slice	7
Berry pie	1 slice	10
Cream pie	1 slice	4
Coconut pie	1 slice	10
Lemon pie	1 slice	7

Source: Bruce S. Fieldman, D.M.D., P.C.

Dental facts.

You've Come a Long Way, Baby: A Look at Pediatric Dentistry

It's such a cheery place. Natural light streams through picture windows, intensifying the already-bright blues, yellows and reds. A pint-sized patient plays a video game in the examining room while her younger sister peers through a child-size telescope at Worcester and beyond. From his hiding place in an overhead examining light, *Sesame Street's* Big Bird winks down at them.

Within this pleasant place cheerful people work and visit—the dentist, who speaks gently and softly; the hygienist, who cracks jokes; the parents, appearing totally relaxed; and the youngsters who play in the waiting room, talking to colorful tropical fish that don't talk back.

Should dentistry be so "laid-back" and comfortable? When does the game end and reality begin? According to Dr. Bruce Fieldman, pediatric dentist and member of the Saint Vincent Medical and Dental Staff, the atmosphere is absolutely essential and pervades every aspect of treatment. "My goals are kids free from fear and kids without cavities," he says, adding, "The physical environment aids in conveying the message that going to the dentist can be pleasant."

Since prevention is the name of this game, Dr. Fieldman likes to see patients as early as 18 months. He teaches proper oral hygiene and good nutrition to parents, then reinforces preventive care with checkups every six months.

"It's sugar, sugar, sugar that causes decay," emphasizes Dr. Fieldman. He points out that the all-American favorite, peanut butter and jelly, is a cavity-causing sandwich containing up to 10 teaspoons of sugar. Twenty seconds after a child eats a peanut butter and jelly sandwich, he says, the bacteria in the mouth combine with the sugar, creating an acid called plaque. When allowed to work into the teeth for 35 minutes, plaque can cause bleeding gums and cavities. How to counter this? Dr. Fieldman recommends offering your child a natural-ground peanut butter sandwich with sliced bananas, a more nutritious snack and better for the teeth.

Sweet drinks, even the natural sugar found in milk, cause a shocking amount of decay in the mouths of babies who continuously nurse on bottles. The syndrome is very common but can be avoided if the dentist sees a child as early as 1½. "I'm astonished when a parent brings in a three-year-old for a first visit with blackened and broken teeth," says Dr. Fieldman.

He recalls one little girl, 2½, running a low-grade fever and eating poorly. "The youngster's top teeth and bottom back teeth were black with decay and one, an empty shell, had broken off following a fall. The bottom front part of her mouth was fine because the tongue naturally protects front teeth." Hospitalized overnight, the little girl's treatment included plastic and silver capping, nerve restoration and silver fillings. If she hadn't received treatment, she would have remained practically toothless until 12 years old, and that would have affected her speech, her permanent teeth and her social development. However, once treated, no permanent harm was done.

Ten Tooth Tips for Parents

- Take your child to the dentist before the age of two.
- Don't allow him to fall asleep with a bottle containing milk, juice, soda or any sweetened liquid.
- Be sure he avoids sweet snacks.
- Clean his teeth and gums after every feeding.
- Read food labels, remembering that sucrose, dextrose, corn syrup and honey are all sugars.
- Offer substitutes like popcorn, nuts, cheese, pizza, fresh vegetables and fresh fruits.
- Use a soft-bristled toothbrush with a small head.
- Use a fluoridated toothpaste approved by the American Dental Association.
- Floss to remove plaque between the teeth and under the gumline.
- Visit the dentist twice a year. Allow the dentist to become your family's partner-in-prevention.

We all know primary teeth are going to fall out, but do we realize how important those teeth are to future dental health? Many remain in the mouth about 12 years," . . . forming holding pillars that enable the jaw to develop correctly and permanent teeth to appear in the proper position." Untreated, primary teeth often lead to misshapen, crooked and discolored permanent teeth.

Fortunately, great strides have been made in methods of prevention and treatment; the use of sealants being the most exciting. A few drops of the liquid plastic applied to newly erupted back molars—". . . very prone to early decay"—seals them against most decay-causing bacteria. An initial application can last as long as 10 years.

Brushing, flossing and fluoride complete pediatric prevention programs. Dr. Fieldman recommends children brush after eating and before bedtime with a soft toothbrush using a fluoride toothpaste, flossing to eliminate the remainder. Fluoride applications are important, he adds, because they harden and strengthen tooth enamel, making teeth more plaque resistant. Fluoride, available by prescription, can also be applied during an office visit.

Following a good pediatric dental prevention program does make a difference. An Associated Press article reports that improved dietary habits, increased use of fluoride and better dental care are believed responsible for a 32 percent decline in tooth decay among American children over the past 10 years. Unfortunately, the article also states children from New England have the worst teeth in the nation, with only 30 percent free of decay compared to children in the Southwest, who are in the 44th percentile.

When parents allow dentists to become partners in prevention, then perhaps more youngsters in New England will become ". . . kids without cavities." And that, of course, would make Dr. Fieldman very happy.

Source: Bruce S. Fieldman, "You've Come a Long Way, Baby: A Look at Pediatric Dentistry," *Outlook* 1 (June 1982): 1, 4. Used by permission.

Dental facts.

Tooth Activities

- *Toothbrush* Cut out a toothbrush shape out of wallpaper
  Paste onto a piece of paper
  Glue dry spaghetti or straw or yarn for bristles
  Paste on hat, eyes, mouth, etc., at will
- *Happy Tooth* Mix white playdough
  Draw basic tooth shape on cardboard
  Push playdough into the shape
  Let dry hard; paint white
  Paste, paint, or draw on a happy face
  If you put a hole in the top when first making, you can hang it on a ribbon for a necklace
- *Decay Monster* Mix green or purple playdough
  Put in bird seed or small gravel or stones
  Shape into any scarey shape you like
  Let dry, when dry add ugly feet and face
- *Songs* Use one you know or add new words to an old song. One possibility is the "Mulberry Bush Song" with the words changed to: "This is the way we brush our teeth after every meal."

Use stories about dentists and teeth; use filmstrips; set up a pretend dentist office for the dolls in the room

Snack Activities

You can find many good, nutritious snack books on the market today. Here are a few of the ideas I have found successful. One note: when introducing a new snack, *never* insist the child eat it all! You are trying to promote new eating habits and allow the child to feel in charge on some decision making. I always tell the children "One bite, it's okay; two bites, it's not so bad; three bites, umm good!" If by three bites, the child hates it, I allow the child to throw it away. Give small samples of new foods and use small dishes.

- *Snack Bugs* Use two crackers; put on a plate, with one as body and one as head
  Put a topping on the crackers: peanut butter, cheese, cold cut
  Add fruit-slice wings: apple, pear, peach, etc.; 2 or 4 wings
  Create a face from raisins, nuts, or pretzel pieces
  Make antenna from pretzels
  Admire and eat

- *Painted Bread* Use slices of white bread as your canvas
  Put milk into little cups; add food coloring to each cup
  Paint with the milk paint on bread; use cotton swabs for brushes
  Let dry and make your sandwich. You can also toast the bread
- *Fruit Ka-Bobs* Cube fruits: peach, pear, apple, watermelon, melon, etc.
  You can add grapes, blueberries, raspberries, etc.
  Let the children spear their own ka-bobs with toothpicks
- *Ka-Bob Dips* Yogurt, lemon instant pudding, vanilla instant pudding
  Dip your ka-bobs and eat
- *Crazy Lunch* Cube cheese, bologna, or spam or ham, fruit slices
  Give the children toothpicks
  Let them choose their own lunch parts and eat
- *Cookie-Cutter Sandwiches* Put out bread, add lunch meat and cheese, open faced
  Hand out small cookie cutters
  The children cut out their fun sandwiches
  Eat; repeat if still hungry
- *Pinwheel Sandwiches* Roll bread with rolling pin
  Spread with peanut butter and favorite go-along
  Cut off crust with plastic knife
  Roll the bread into a jelly roll
  Toothpick the roll every few centimeters
  Slice between the toothpicks
  Place on a plate; eat
- *Outer Space Saucers* Cut English muffins in half
  Add tomato sauce
  Add pizza cheese
  Decorate the space craft with bits of hamburg, sliced peppers, pepperoni, etc.
  Bake at 400° for ten minutes; eat
- *Fish Ka-Bobs* Cook prepackaged fish ka-bobs and potato puffs as per packages
  Let the children spear the fish and potatoes with toothpicks
  Dip in ketchup, tarter sauce, or barbeque sauce
  Eat and enjoy
- *Fruit Juice Pops* Mix the children's favorite juices
  Pour into ice cube trays
  Add a half popsickle stick to each cube

Freeze; eat and enjoy
Alternatives: Mix and freeze instant pudding
add blueberry to each cube
add cherry juice to the juice mix

- *Pickle Alligators* Buy whole pickles (small), green olives, raisins, carrots
Slice a mouth in the front of the pickle
Toothpick the pimento from the olive into the mouth or toothpick the whole olive to the pickle as the head
Toothpick olives for the legs
Toothpick raisins for the eyes and nose
Cut carrot wedge and toothpick in as tail
Admire and eat
- *Vegetables and Dip* Mix sour cream or yogurt with dry vegetable soup mix
Wash, slice, and cut to bite-size favorite vegetables: carrots, peppers, cauliflower, broccoli, cherry tomatoes, cucumbers, etc.

In general, popcorn, low-sugar cereals, pretzels, vegetables, fruits, crackers with peanut butter/cheese or cheese spread, peanuts or other nuts make great snacks for children. As always, snacks should be eaten sitting down and never running about the house or yard. For safety's sake.

Caution should also be used to see that all toothpicks are removed from foods before eating. Teachers should be conscious of and respect any philosophical or religious dietary prohibitions. Keep in mind also foods that children may have an allergic reaction to: milk, nuts, citrus fruits, chocolate, and wheat products, for example.

Snacks That Are Good to Eat and Good for You

Nutritious Snacks

tomato slices
*carrot sticks
pears
cucumber slices
pepper slices
fruit in the can (juice pack)
bananas
pretzels
pineapple
cheese chunks
hard-boiled eggs
*celery sticks
melons
grapes
cauliflower
strawberries
bread sticks
**popcorn
grapefruit
meat cubes (spam, bologna, etc.)
crackers
cherries
peaches
orange wedges
radishes
tangerines
apples
unsweetened dry cereal
pickles
plums
***peanuts

Raisins are nutritious but can contribute to cavities in teeth because they are sticky. Allow children to have them at breakfast so they can brush teeth immediately after eating.

Avoid sugared products and products that rely heavily on additives and artificial colorings. Limit salt intake.

Other names for sugar: sucrose, fructose, corn syrup, dextrose. On packaging, the higher up on the list of ingredients, the higher the percentage of the ingredient. *Read packages. Less is best!*

***Beware:** Carrots can be dangerous with toddlers. Make sure that they are cut thinly and long and the children are sitting down under supervision when eating. *Never* allow the children to run about while eating.

**Use *hulless* popcorn only!

*****Avoid** small, round, and tube-like shapes for young children because they are easy to choke on. For example, avoid hot dogs with skins as well as chunky cut carrots, celery, and hard vegetables.

QUESTIONS FOR REVIEW

1. What is the most effective way to teach children to overcome fear?
2. Name two of the four methods that help children become less fearful.
3. The first thing that every child should be taught is ____.
4. What is the easiest way for a child to learn a telephone number?
5. The first thing for a child to do in an emergency is to ____________.
6. What are the four *W*'s?
7. Should children practice first aid on each other?
8. Why is it necessary to change the situations when teaching a young child first aid?
9. Name some follow-up activities after the child learns first aid.
10. Does a child have to answer the telephone's questions?
11. What is the first aid for nosebleeds that you would teach a child?
12. Why would you teach dental care as part of this first aid chapter?
13. What kind of toothbrush is best for young children and why?
14. Who or what is Chef Combo?
15. Why analyze television ads for cereal with children? Aren't the children too young?
16. Name three nutritious snacks.
17. Name two highly sugared cereals and two cereals that are good for children.
18. Even a young child can learn to call on the telephone for help by dialing ____________.

CHAPTER 4

Home Safety

SAFETY IN THE HOME

Safety at home is very important for young children because so much of their life is spent at home. Young children are much more likely to harm themselves or get into dangerous situations at home than anywhere else.

Look around the home! Windows that open, medicines that look like candy, cleaning fluids that might taste good, cords that can be pulled, funny little holes in the wall, toilets that are full of water and swish so pleasantly, chairs to climb, and many other things could appeal to children for many reasons. When you add to these dangers the stove, the possibility of a fire or gas explosion, and strangers on the telephone or at the door, it is easy to see how the house can be a dangerous place!

Much can be done with children to help turn a potentially dangerous place back into our peaceful haven. The adult needs to be firm and to explain the dangers clearly and specifically for children. What adults say must make sense, and the reasons must be clear or children will not listen or retain the warnings.

It is important that parents teach children how to use the telephone to get proper help for home emergencies. Keep a list of emergency help telephone numbers by the telephone. Practice role plays of home emergencies and help children check the emergency list for the proper person to call in each case.

Poison

First, it is time to dispel the myth that a child who is being watched cannot ingest poison. It is true that children need close supervision at a young age, but it is also nearly impossible to watch any active child twenty-four hours a day with constant vigilance. When you add to the situation more children or a stove

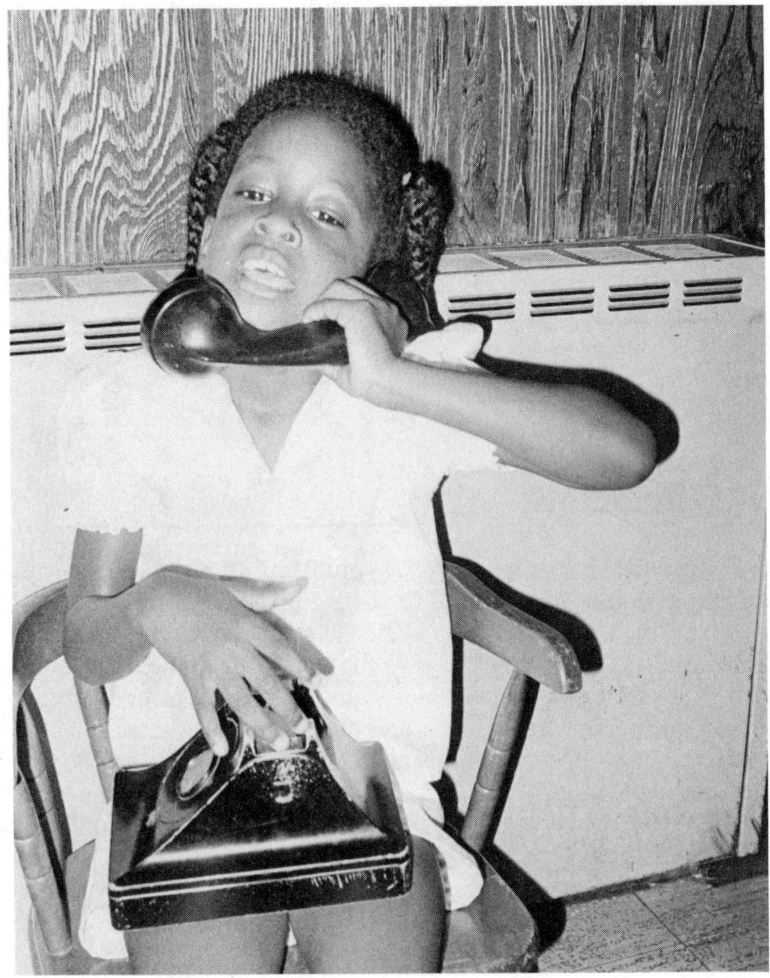

Learning how to telephone for help is as vital for the child as learning how to telephone home. An important follow-up skill to teach is that the child has the right to hang up when feeling threatened.

that has just buzzed for dinner, you increase the potential for danger. Locking away the poisons is not enough. What happens at someone else's home? What happens when dad leaves the oil for the lawnmower out for a minute?

What happens when the child figures out how to open that safety bottle? Be aware that "Child resistant caps are not as safe as you think. Parents are being lulled into a false sense of security about child-proof bottle caps with tragic results, according to Duke University researcher, Dr. W. Kip Viscusi. He claims

Safety latches and caps alone are not effective in safeguarding young children. Children need to recognize materials that are poisonous. Mr. Yuk quickly lets a child know that something is dangerous.

manufacturers' claims are misleading that poisonings have decreased since the bottle caps' introduction in 1972 . . . it is the decrease in the baby boom . . . that has led to an overall decrease in poisonings. In 1972, 40 percent of all aspirin poisonings were due to bottle cap misuse, but the figure jumped to 73 percent in 1978. The reason: Consumers 'have been lulled into a less safety conscious mode of behavior by the existence of the safety caps.'"[1] Aside from the safety cap issue within your home, what could happen when a child gets into a purse or a medicine chest in someone's home if he or she does not know about poison safety? You need to do more than use safety caps and lock up poisons and medicines; you cannot rely on these methods alone.

---

1. Central Massachusetts Health Care, Inc., *Your Health & Fitness* (Highland Park, Il.: Curriculum Innovations, Inc., June/July 1984), 14.

The technique successful with many classes is an aggressive poison campaign. Various safety programs have used the Mr. Yuk symbol over the years. Mr. Yuk is a sticker—green with an unhappy face. The children learn that this symbol is a sign of danger; whatever is in a container with a Mr. Yuk on it is *dangerous* and *not to be touched* because it can hurt them by making them sick or burning them. The children discuss with the adult why they do not like being sick. They then go around the school or home putting stickers on all the containers with contents that are bad for them; they discuss why each one is bad as they stick on Mr. Yuk. As a further precaution for areas without Mr. Yuk, children are asked to think about the kinds of things that were bad and see if they could find them or know them without Mr. Yuk. They are also warned about the dangers of putting even a soda bottle in their mouth without first checking with an adult. After all, someone could have put something other than soda into the bottle. This is a good role-play situation.

The children can then make a big Mr. Yuk. A certificate for poison knowledge should be awarded at the end of this content area.

Parents should be made aware of the efforts about Mr. Yuk. Send home extra Mr. Yuk symbols for the parents to use. Any plain green stickers can be made into Mr. Yuk with a marker. Parents also should be reminded to lock away dangerous detergents, medicines, beauty products (nail polish remover, astringents, etc.), and liquor.

Alcohol should never be given to children! A young child can die from drinking a relatively small dose of alcohol. If you give children tacit permission to drink by laughing and letting them sample a drink, you are setting up the possibility of tragedy when the child gets a hold of alcohol someday when you are not looking. Alcohol consumption also can cause minimal damage to the young child's developing brain. Even a small amount of alcohol can cause dizziness and loss of coordination. This combination easily could lead to a nasty fall for a child.

Fire

Smoke in the middle of the night! Do you know what to do? Without practice in how to behave during a fire emergency, the chances of a child getting out alive are limited. Tragedies occur because a child went back into a burning building for a toy or a dog. Tragedies occur because an older child or parent goes back in for a smaller child who often is already out of the house. Good planning can avoid such needless tragedies.

Even though children are fearful about what happens during a fire, they like fire trucks and fire fighters. Using these together, it is easy to motivate children to learn fire safety. A visit to a local fire station is a good beginning for a young child learning fire safety. Always call ahead to arrange the visit.

Fire Chief Lory Russell of Leicester, Massachusetts, has been giving tours to preschoolers for years. The first thing he tells them is to leave a building that is on fire! Get out and don't go back for anything! Many fire officials suggest that a family designate a place outside away from the building, at which to meet in a fire emergency. It thus is known immediately if anyone is missing, and the spot becomes a focal point to keep the little ones in one place.

Fire drills are very important. Without practice, the child may panic and hide in closet or do something else that would be deadly. "Conduct a family fire drill, carefully explaining what the child should do. If the fire occurs at night, he should roll out of bed, crawl to the door, feel the door with the back of his hand. If the door is hot, he should immediately try to climb out a window. If he can't safely jump out the window, he should drape a sheet over the window over the windowsill to alert firefighters that he is trapped and then stay on the floor."[2] If the child can feel no heat at the door, the child should crawl out of the house as he did during the drill and go immediately to the prearranged meeting place and stay there. "*Special Home Safety Packet for Your Family:* The National Fire Protection Association will send you a pamphlet on fire safety and exit drills in the home to share with your children. Simply send a business-sized, stamped, self-addressed envelope to 'EDITH' (FC), Publication Sale, NFPA, Batterymarch Park, Quincy, MA 02269."[3]

Adults should not only conduct fire drills regularly but should role play how the child would and should respond to different fire emergencies. Some situations to role play include the following.

Examples

A fire comes in the night, should you get Mommy? What should you do?

The stairs are on fire now; what should you do?

You are at the meeting place, but no one else is there; what should you do?

You are home alone; should you wait til Mom comes home or call for help or go to your meeting place or a neighbors?

These questions need to be answered by the family as to the best family decision. The rules of thumb should be common sense and good fire safety sense.

Children also need to know what to do if they catch fire. Instinct and panic tell them to run, but this is wrong! Actor Dick van Dyke does a one-minute television spot on fire safety in which he tells children to "Stop! drop! and roll!" He acts out these movements with paper flames that come off as he rolls. This role play works with classes well. The children all remember what to do if they or someone else catch fire and they love practicing the procedure. The little

2. Terri Fields, "Teach Your Kids to Protect Themselves," *Family Circle* (March 6, 1984), 50.
3. Fields.

flames can be made of cardboard with red glitter. Use masking tape to hold them onto the children.

Children need to learn about safety and stoves—the kitchen stove and also wood-burning stoves. Wood-burning stoves are often located in the middle of a room and thus are likely to be touched or bumped into. They do not have insulated steel around them as does a kitchen stove. A child thus could get a bad burn from a wood burner. The safety note about keeping pot handles angled in on a stove is good advice.

Fireplaces can be even more hazardous than stoves. A fireplace should be properly screened to prevent sparks from popping out at a child. Children should be taught to sit away from the fireplace. Screens get hot and can burn little fingers. A sturdy screen is important to insure stability if children bump into it.

Be careful what you burn in the fireplace. Both green wood and seasoned wood may have poison ivy still clinging. Remove all ivy, because if burned it can cause poison ivy reactions in the face and inside the throat and lungs. Never burn painted wood or colored pages from newspapers and magazines. These release lead into the air when burned, which can be very hazardous to children.

Keep matches away from the fireplace to eliminate the temptation to light a fire. Cigarette lighters and matches should always be kept out of children's reach. Teaching match safety should include having the children give matches to an adult anytime they find them. A positive verbal response by the adult should always follow this action. Children should know they will be praised for good match safety. Role playing about what to do with matches should be part of this content area. Candle safety should be mentioned; children find candles attractive, and many parents entertain with them. Hanging over candles can be dangerous because hair catches fire easily.

Making fire hats, badges, and hoses are fun activities and allow children the opportunity to role play on their own the fire rules. Some fire safety songs and finger plays such as those in Figures 4.3 and 4.4 at the end of this chapter text also facilitate learning and retention.

Natural gas has been a boon as a heating fuel and energy source. The fuel is odorless and quiet. It can also explode. A smell similar to rotten eggs is added to the fuel in many areas so the gas can be easily detected if it is in the air. If you smell the rotten egg smell, you are supposed to leave the building immediately; do *not* switch a light switch; do *not* use the telephone! A small electrical spark that sets your phone in motion is enough to set off an explosion! Go to a neighbors and call the gas company. They are equipped to handle an emergency. You need to know about the gas smell even if you do not heat with gas. Recent developments have shown that gas sometimes travels up water pipes to nearby houses if there is a leak in the gas pipe even two or three houses away. If you smell the gas smell even if you don't heat with gas, Get out! Call the gas company. Contact your local gas company to get a free card with a scratch-and-sniff spot that helps children learn the gas smell.

Water Safety

Summer is for swimming and boating. This is also the time that water-related accidents are at their peak. A child does not need a pond to drown in; a dishpan full of water is enough to drown a young child. *Never leave a child unattended in or near water!* Do not leave to answer the telephone! Do not leave until you get the children out of the water and bring them in with you. This action is wetter on the floor but safer for the children. Children should be taught *not* to go in the water to save another child. Water safety instructors say that even a child who is a good swimmer can drown trying to save another child. A drowning person does not think or act logically. A drowning person will try to climb onto the saver. A drowning person has incredible strength and can actually strangle the saver in an attempt to get out of water. Children, including older children, should be taught to throw a float, stick, or other object into the water that the victim can hold onto while you pull them in or go get help. A child is much more likely to save a brother, sister, or friend in this manner.

In winter, outdoor water safety becomes ice safety. A water rescue, however, may still be necessary if a child falls through the ice into the water. The best way to help such a victim is to lay on the ice and hand out a stick, or towel, for the victim to hold. *Never* jump in and save the victim.

In all water-related dangers, well-thought-out plans are the best deterrents to preventing tragedy. Learning to float can save a child's life. Talk to the children at the start of each season. Remind them about the safety rules for summer or winter. In few cases will a child stop to remember what they learned an entire season ago.

Swimming and Diving. Have the children relate swimming and diving safety rules, such as

- "Learn to swim well enough to survive in an emergency.
- Never swim alone.
- Swim only in supervised areas. . . .
- Learn the simple and safe reaching rescues. . . .
- Stay out of the water when overheated and immediately after eating.
- Stay out of the water during electrical storms.
- Do not substitute inflated tubes, air mattresses, or artificial supports for swimming ability.
- Call for help only when you really need it."[4]

Ice Skating. "Because of currents, the ice thickness on rivers and streams varies. A parent or other adult should always determine the safety of the ice before

4. American National Red Cross, *Basic Aid Training* (Washington, D.C.: ARC, 1980), 3.

anyone goes on it."[5] It is important that children role play what to do before skating or ice fishing or even walking on ice. Accidents can happen to anyone, anywhere, but accidents can be survived if the people know how to handle the situations.

Ice Rescue. If you should fall through the ice, don't panic. Keep calm. Don't try to climb out. Extend both arms along the surface and kick vigorously. This will help to lift your body forward onto solid ice. Then roll to safety.

Again, to test the children's knowledge of these skills, role play situations and judge their answers as to their readiness to go on to the next area. A certificate for water safety is a reward for learning well. A practical test in a pool or pond can also show the adults if the children know the water rules.

Your local YMCA, YWCA, Boys' Club, Girls' Club, and American Red Cross offer excellent beginner swimming classes with qualified water safety instructors. These courses are a good place for children to learn water safety while learning to float and swim.

Household Items and Appliances

Other areas of danger in the house are electrical appliances. Young children are curious and love to try new things and investigate nooks and crannies. A dryer that opens frontward can be a danger as a hiding place or a closet. Safety knobs help when children are younger but are of little use when children get older. Taking a child on a periodic house inspection when you ask what items could be dangerous and why could save a child's life. Explaining each kitchen utensil, including the knives, also could keep a curious child from self-investigations. Adults can teach children to cook at a young age and let them use a sharp knife—under supervision. A sharp knife works better, with less chance of cutting, and children learn that the knife is used only for certain jobs and only with an adult. Even preschool children can use sharp knives for cutting under proper supervision. Of course, always store the knives out of sight and where the access is limited.

Toilets can be dangerous to young children. They are the right size for a child to stick a head in and get stuck. Drowning occurs as the child struggles. The bathroom with its tub and toilet should be included on the safety tour.

Small appliances such as mixers, toasters, and blenders need to be explained and used with young children so they understand both their uses and their dangers. The more the children know about these items, the less likely they are to get hurt. Microwave ovens are a newer appliance for which safety rules also need to be laid down.

---

5. American Red Cross, 23.

All electrical appliances should be left unplugged after use. This good practice can save a child from shock. Children should also learn that electrical appliances are *never* put near water.

Electrical cords and outlets need to also be explained to children. Most area electric companies offer free coloring books and other materials that explain electricity. The pictures help explain how electricity works. The clear caps that cover electrical outlets are preferable because they attract less attention than the white or brown while keeping little hands out.

This chapter has covered a lot of material quickly, but the information is important for young children to understand. Knowledge of how things work and why they have safety rules should help the children avoid misusing the materials around them. Understanding takes a lot of the mystery away. You can take more time and add projects on these areas as necessary. When the

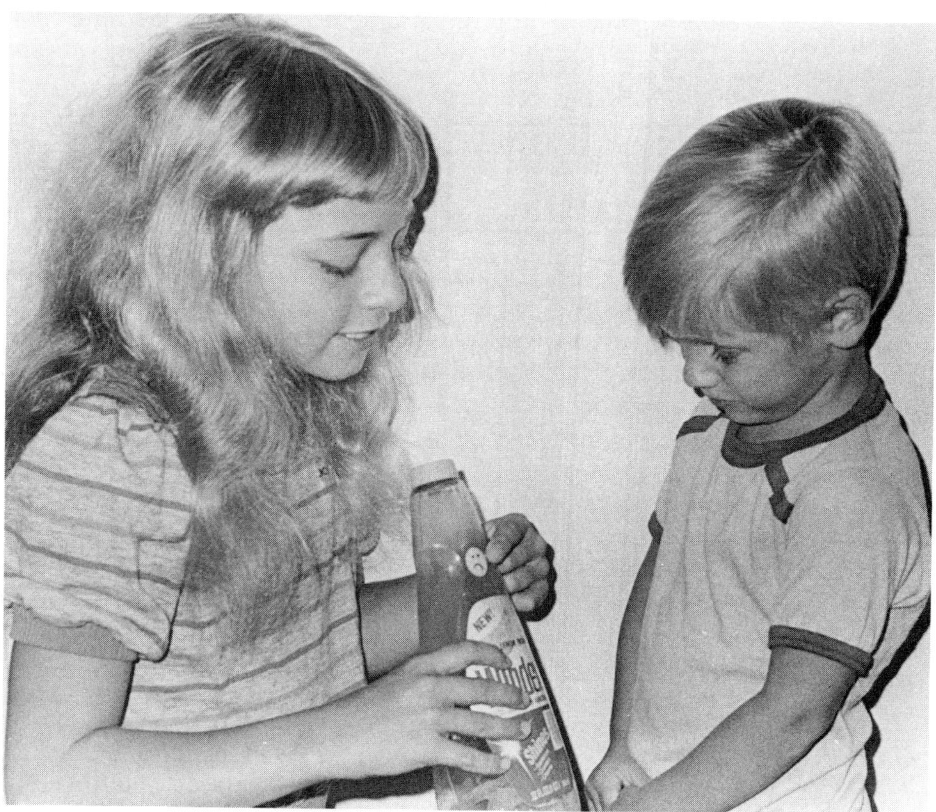

Older siblings can help reinforce the importance of Mr. Yuk around the house.

children can answer "what if" situations correctly, place a sticker on Home Safety on their charts and move ahead to the next content area, Street Smarts.

The last two areas of home safety, the telephone and door safety, are covered in Chapter 6 on victimization prevention.

The next few pages list some materials you can find when you take your safety tour of the house and yard or the day-care center and yard. Remember to discuss with the children what they are looking for and why these things can be dangerous. Try to get each child to answer individually. Use Mr. Yuk stickers freely when first doing a tour and remember to do follow-up tours and ask periodically about specific items seen on the tour. Another good follow-up is to make a giant Mr. Yuk that all the children color; leave him up as a poster. Again, using the Red Cross Batman posters is an effective review. You can also acquire free handouts about home safety from many insurance companies, poison control centers, the fire department, and public health departments. These materials can be sent home to parents as reminders; they are interesting reading for anyone who works with children.

Common sense is the important ingredient for learning about safety at home. A little planning can avoid many accidents and tragedies.

HOUSE SAFETY TOUR

Taking a tour of the house can be easy. Run off a master diagram of each room for each child. As you and the children walk through the house, draw or write down each potentially hazardous item. After the tour, the diagrams can then be taped together into a miniature house shape. You can easily do this with preschool children.

Potential Hazards

Kitchen: stoves, refrigerators, small appliances and overhanging cords from these appliances, frayed cords, knives, glasses, junk drawers, cleaners and detergents in or under the sink area, kitchen tools, spills on the floor

Stairways: barriers like gates that bunch, poor lighting, loose treads, lack of banisters, items on the treads

Bathroom: radios and appliances in the bathroom, razors and razor blades, deodorant sprays, nail clippers, medications in the medicine chest if unlocked, tubs without nonskid surfaces, toilets, toilet cleaners and rim cleaners, glasses and glass bottles, rugs that slip.

Bedroom/parlor: night-lights in the bedrooms, pillows in baby's crib, heavy lamps on small tables, perfumes, aftershaves, beauty creams, nail polish and remov-

FIGURE 4.1
House diagram.

ers, improperly hung plants, poisonous house plants, fireplace and equipment for same, stereo and television equipment, hard candies in a candy dish, pocketbooks, heating outlets like radiators, grills, woodburners, aquariums

Attic: unlocked old trunks, old clothes or plastic bags (suffocation), uneven or weak support flooring, unlocked windows

Cellar/garage: paints, turpentine, gasoline, gasoline-filled lawnmowers, nails, screws and power tools, stored windows, lawn tools, clippers, bug or rat poisons, fishing gear, work out machinery, electrical boxes

Every room: electrical outlets, old or frayed cords and overloaded outlets, hanging cords and cords under rugs, uncovered outlets, unscreened and broken windows, unlocked windows on second and higher floors, lead paint, electrical appliances or cords without UL approval, unlocked refrigerators or trunks

Yard: plants; lawn mowers, especially right after using (burn danger is very high); tools left out; improperly maintained decks; railingless porches or stairs; slippery sidewalks, especially in winter; hornets or bees nesting near the house or in lawn furniture; improperly maintained yard toys—swings, climbers, tree houses, bicycles, and unsecured swing sets that can tip over; toys with sharp edges—trucks, fences

From hobbies: sewing needles and pins, sewing machines; glues, especially crazy glue (keep the antidote on hand); photography. Many chemicals are dangerous; think about your hobby as a potential danger and then think how you can teach the child or better secure your materials to reduce danger.

Potentially dangerous items that may be found anywhere in a home include:

Tools: scissors; knives; nail files; nail clippers; nut crackers and picks; stapler and staples; tacks; nails; screwdrivers; batteries, especially small disc-shaped ones; pliers

Odd items: balloons, toothpicks, flashlights, light bulbs, buttons, pins, clips, matches, half-empty glasses, golf balls, ant cups, liquor in unsecured cabinets or left out on a table

Special Addition to House Tour

Driveway: The car can be an extremely dangerous object even when parked safely in the driveway. Keep doors locked at all times. Do not let the children play in the car. Do not let the children play on or under the car. Keep the car in park and keep the emergency brake on if children ever use the driveway. It is also advisable to hang up your keys out of reach instead of leaving them about the house when you are not using the car.

A tour can easily be taken through a day-care center or preschool where the children can look for hazards that might be around. Obviously, a good day-care center has taken care of hazards, but the tour reinforces the need for children to look and become aware.

DANGEROUS PLANTS

Many common plants are dangerous; children should be taught *never* to taste or eat any plant. Many plants look similar, such as a blueberry and a dogwood bush berry. Both are blue and one bears fruit right after the other. A rule of thumb is that *no berry, mushroom, or vegetable* should ever be picked without an adult present!

Another problem for young children is their perception of animals. They often think that if a plant or berry is safe for an animal, then it is safe for them. Birds can eat some berries that are poisonous to people. Explain this to children and have them draw pictures to show what birds eat and what people eat. You can obtain a good book about poisonous plants from any library and a listing of local poisonous plants from your county extension service.

Plants are a part of everyday life, inside the house and out. Many common plants are hazardous, and young children should be taught not to taste them.

Here is a list of a few common poisonous plants. Check your locale for a more complete listing.

In the house: dieffenbachia, hyacinth, philodendron, narcissus, amarylis, glory lily, crown-of-thorns
Christmas greens: boxwood, English ivy, bittersweet, holly and its berries, mistletoe yew, and Jerusalem cherry
Hallucinogenics: Marijuana, morning glory, poppy, nutmeg
Outdoor plants: azalea, rhododendron, clematis, lily of the valley, golden chain, hydrangea, laurel, mountain laurel, tansy, rhubarb, tomato greens, foxglove, bleeding heart, mustard, horsechestnut, and many more
Native and wild plants: baneberry, black cherry, black locust, false hellebore, mushrooms, nightshade, hemlock, snake root, jimsonweed, chinaberry, poison ivy, poison sumac, poison oak, and more

Again, you cannot watch all children at all times. The best protection is to teach the children to leave plants, even garden plants, alone unless with an adult. Another reason not to pick garden plants without an adult is the possibility that the plants are covered with poisonous insecticides or herbicides.

Often, these poisons must wear off and cannot be washed off. You should know what you put on your garden plants; follow poison package directions carefully and always wash fresh produce well. Be careful where and how you dispose of any garden and lawn chemicals.

COMMON HOUSEHOLD POISONS

Keep near the telephone the number for the nearest poison center. Keep ipecac on hand for any poison emergency (available at low cost at any drug store). *Never* store any poisonous material in a container other than the one it came in; for example, never store poison in a soda or other bottle a child is used to touching. Keep poisons locked up and out of reach. Put a Mr. Yuk stickers on all containers *before* you lock them up so the child knows what they are and why they are dangerous. Common household poisons include:

aspirin, acetaminophen and all aspirin substitutes
vitamins (more than one)
alcohol
after-shave and perfume
antihistamines
carbon tetrachloride
bleach
cigarettes
diet pills
deodorants, hair dyes
insecticides, repellents
iron tablets
oil
lighter fluid
wart remover
waxes, car polishes
toilet bowl cleaner
metal polish
laxatives
liniment
permanent markers, liquid mistake removers
mothballs, flakes
nail polish and remover
naphthalene
paregoric
prescription drugs (When was the last time you cleaned these out? Should be cleaned out yearly)
sedatives, sleeping pills
varnish
corn remover
polishes, detergents
lye
oven cleaner
scouring powder
mineral oil
kerosene

Lock up all poisons. Put a Mr. Yuk sticker on all poisons. Be prepared!

LEAD POISONING UPDATE

Many people believe that lead poisoning is not an important issue now that most states have banned the use of lead paint in any building with children. The fact is that lead poisoning is again on the rise. Few pediatricians are testing young children, and few parents are taking advantage of free testing from local public health programs. People feel the threat is over.

What is causing the upswing in cases of lead poisoning? Causative factors include:

Air pollution: Lead from emissions has to settle somewhere, and dirt is where it lands. Who often plays in dirt? Young children. Polluted air also lands in dust in homes.

Old lead water pipes: These aging pipes are depositing their lead into our water supply.

Improperly glazed ceramics: Drinking anything from these containers, especially acidic fruit juices, will yield lead.

Improver removal of leaded paint in homes: As people fix up old homes or add on, they scrape, burn, or sand off old paint, often while children are around. Lead particles in the air and dust in the home are almost totally absorbed by children under six and by pregnant women. This absorption can be enough to cause a tragedy.

Improperly tested water supplies, especially wells: Underground water needs to be tested periodically to insure that mineral and lead contents have not risen to a dangerous level.

Who is at risk? Lead poisoning is not good for anyone, but children under six, for physiological reasons, absorb lead at a much faster rate and are, therefore, at the top level of risk. Pregnant women are also at a high risk level because lead crosses the placenta and is absorbed by the fetus.

What are the signs of lead poisoning? The poisoned child may be listless, appear a bit slow, and usually display other subtle signs that can be easily mistaken for flu or a cold.

How do you determine if a child has lead poisoning? A simple blood test—just a prick on the finger—is sufficient to enable a qualified person to check for lead poisoning. Most public health facilities offer free screening. Many nursery schools and day-care centers have taken a leadership role in alerting parents and making the screening available at the preschool.

What can happen if lead poisoning goes undetected? A child with lead poisoning can suddenly slump into a coma and even die.

Can lead poisoning be treated? Yes, but the further advanced the case, the more painful and prolonged is the treatment. Ask any nurse, doctor, or parent who has been part of the treatment on a severely poisoned child and they will tell you it is a terrible ordeal. Prevention is the best policy. Many physicians recommend blood tests once or twice a year. Ask your physician.

Some children in class may seem to be retarded but in fact are suffering from lead poisoning from peeling lead paint they have ingested. Once treated, these children may be average and above average in ability. Take the time to get blood tests for your children and alert the parents of the children in your care. While we work on air, water, and other pollutions, let's keep the children safe!

Lead Poisoning Fact Sheet

IT IS ON THE RISE

PEOPLE MOST AT RISK:
1. Pregnant women and fetus
2. Ages one through four
3. Then ages four through five
4. Then ages six until physiological changes make it less of a risk due to a lower absorbtion rate.

CAUSES: Lead in the air and soil (from pollution and leaded gasoline)
Leafy green vegetables grown in affected soil
Lead paint chips or sanding particles

EFFECT ON CHILD: 5 mg to 15 mg—some neurological effects.
30 mg—*Toxic level*—more damage to brain. The higher the count, the less likely the chance of reversibility.
Most severe point—seizure to coma to death; if the child lives through at this point, the child is left with handicaps (speech, hearing, and neurological).
New studies show that even a low-level exposure over a period of time can be damaging.

TREATMENT: The sooner caught, the better the chances for reversal. Injections into the muscle and bloodstream of a lead-attracting substance and periods in the hospital are usual parts of treatment, which may take a long time. Speak to a doctor for a more scientific explanation. The treatment is not easy and is painful.

LEAD CROSSES PLACENTA to the unborn fetus and is suspected of causing stillborn births in high dosages. Pregnant women should beware of leaded substances.

PREVENTIONS: A simple, painless, and usually free *blood test*
Public *awareness* and *education*
Hand washing after playing on floors or in dirt
Removing children from home when stripping or sanding paint
Political lobbying for *testing* of all preschool children
Political lobbying for a *ban* on leaded gasoline (as in Europe)

FIGURE 4.2
Lead poisoning fact sheet.

QUICK WAYS TO CHILDPROOF THE HOME

1. Hang plants out of reach.
2. Put safety covers (clear) into electrical outlets. Remove cords from view.
3. Remove knives, nail clippers, scissors, and the like from view and reach.
4. Keep all plastic bags locked up, away from view.
5. Remove dangling table cloths.
6. Put hook-and-eye locks on the cellar door and medicine closet—up high.
7. Secure all medications, detergents, and such up high and out of reach and sight.
8. Keep cigarettes, lighters, matches, and other smoking materials up and away from young children.
9. Put a lock or hook-and-eye on the outside of the bathroom door to keep toddlers out.
10. Store plastics and pans under the sink so if children get there, they can safely play.
11. Unplug all small appliances when not in use.
12. Walk through the house and imagine you are only two or three feet tall. Remove any dangers at that height.
13. Secure bookcases and potentially harmful furniture that could easily tip if the child climbed up.
14. Keep the microwave unplugged or secured so little hands cannot get burned.
15. Put a lock on your deep freeze.
16. Keep an eye on the washer and dryer if you cannot lock the door to the laundry area.
17. Do not put heavy objects on light pieces of furniture. Televisions, stereos, and other such items should be on sturdy pieces so they will not fall on the child if the table is bumped.
18. *Learn to say "No" and mean it* when the child touches potentially dangerous items or materials you do not want touched. It is not necessary to remove everything, but a bit of prevention can make a huge difference in enjoying your little ones without nagging.
19. *Lock up* firearms and ammunition. Lock up each item in a separate place to insure against unauthorized use. *Always unload* firearms and remove the firing pin before locking away. Store ammunition in a separate location.
20. Swimming pools: With the increase in the number of backyard pools has come an increase in drownings. Fence in your pool. Tie up the ladder securely. Practice floating techniques with your children. Enroll your children in swimming lessons by the age of five. You can buy an inexpensive alert ball that sets off an alarm the minute the water is disturbed. Keep small kiddie pools empty when an adult is not present to supervise.
21. Hot water: Turn down the thermostat on your water heater. Water heated too hot wastes money and energy and can cause terrible scalds on young

children. Set the water at 120° F. This temperature is hot enough and eliminates burn risk.

22. Bathtubs: *Never* leave a child unattended in the tub. One quarter of all children's drownings occur in the tub.
23. Carpeting: Secure loose carpeting with a rubber undersheet or tacking, especially on stairs and slippery flooring.
24. Stairs: Be sure the stairs are well-lit at night and have a railing that is secure and reachable. Do not use the stairs for storage. Keep them free of all obstructions.
25. Fire extinguisher: Buy at least one for your home. They are inexpensive and invaluable for grease fires and other difficult fires. *Teach the family how to use the extinguisher.*
26. Fire exits: If you only have one exit from your second floor, buy a safety chain ladder. Secure it upstairs and practice its use with family members.
27. Floors: Do not wax floors if you have young children who are learning to crawl or walk. The slippery wax can cause them to fall. New floor coverings are available that are shiny but do not leave the floor slippery.

Never Play with Matches
(sung to: *Frere Jacques*)

Never, never play with matches,
if you do, if you do
you might burn your fingers,
you might burn your fingers,
that won't do, that won't do.
by Leora Grecian, San Bernardino, California

Firefighters
(sung to: *Pop Goes the Weasel*)

Down the street the engine goes
The firemen fight the fire
Up the ladder with their hose
Out goes the fire
by Mrs. Gary McNitt, Adrian, Michigan

I Am a Fireman
(sung to: *I'm a Little Teapot*)

I am a fireman, dressed in red,
With my fire hat on my head
I can drive the fire truck, fight fire too!
And help to make things safe for you.
by Judy Hall, Wytheville, Virginia

Other ideas:

Fire fighting

Color a stove or washing machine carton and decorate with fire swatches.
Use an old vacuum cleaner hose for a pretend fire hose.
Have a fire safety inspection.
Have practice fire drills.
Make a fire truck out of a cardboard box and paste on wheels.
Read *Smokey the Bear.*
Visit a fire station or have a visit from a firefighter.

Water safety

Get inexpensive Red Cross Namu the Whale posters.
Go to a swimming pool and have a water safety instructor show the children some safety techniques, especially what to do if they fall in.

Medicine safety

Talk about who should give medications, including vitamins.
Visit a drug store and meet the pharmacists; they can show the children safety caps and explain why they are put on bottles of medication.

FIGURE 4.3

Some fire safety songs and other suggestions. (Songs from Piggyback Songs *and* More Piggyback Songs, *compiled by Jean Warren. Everett, Wash.: Totline Press, Warren Publishing House. Used with permission.)*

Police or Fire Hat

Blue paper.
Mount on hatboard.
Paste silver badge on front.

Two paper plates.
Staple together with top one on a fold.
Color red. Punch holes for ties.

Fire Fighters Hose

Color toilet paper roll red or black for hose.
Paste in blue crepe paper for water.

Police Badge

Cardboard covered with silver foil.

Use black marker for name and badge number.

Punch holes and string yarn.

Pretend Walkie-Talkie

Cut out cardboard to shape. Cover with foil. Paste on black speaker. Put on two black switches with paper fasteners.

Used by police and fire fighters to communicate.

Pretend Fire for Safety Game

Cut out cardboard fire. Color it yellow or cover it with silver foil.

Squiggle glue.
Sprinkle red glitter.

Put masking tape behind the fire to hold it to the child.

Make a Firetruck

Set two rows of chairs back to back with two chairs up front for the drivers.

The children all sit on the truck to sing their fire safety songs. They get off, run with hoses to put out fires and run back to the truck.

FIGURE 4.4
Fire safety games.

INFANT AND TODDLER EQUIPMENT GUIDES

1. *Changing tables: Never* leave a child alone, even for a moment. Secure child with the table's safety belt, but do not rely on it to keep child there.
2. *Bounce chairs* with or without casters: They often tip quite easily. Be careful to see that the child does not have to maneuver from an area with a rug onto a different surface or level.
3. *Toy chests:* Remove the covers or replace with a stay-open safety latch to keep the lid from falling and hurting a child.
4. *Playpens: Keep sides up.* When down, the mesh sides can smother a child snuggled in the corner. Also do not place large stuffed toys or big toys in playpens so children do not use them as footholds to climb out and fall. *Do not use wooden extending play corrals;* many children have gotten their heads caught between the wooden slats, with tragic results.
5. *Baby gates* and *barriers: Beware!* These are not foolproof or all safe. They are only temporary stops to a determined child. Adult supervision is still needed. *Watch* wooden extending gates; children have gotten necks caught in them. They are not recommended.
6. *Cribs*
   a. *Make sure* corner posts are less than 5/8 of an inch high.
   b. *Slats* should be less than 2 3/8 inches apart and secure.
   c. *Head and footboards* should not have slits big enough to catch a head or hand.
   d. *Mattress* should fit snugly, allowing *no room* for baby to slip.
   e. *Bumpers* should fit snugly; they should have at least six ties, all tied securely (trim the edges if too long).
   Remove bumpers as soon as the child can pull up to a standing position so the child cannot climb up them and fall.
   f. *Place crib away* from windows, drapes with cords, curtains, electrical outlets, and cords.
   g. *Never* hang stringed objects in crib (possible strangulation).
   h. *Lock* side rail as soon as the child can stand (up position).
   i. *Make sure* all screws and bolts are tightly secured; check periodically.
   j. *Do not* put pillows into a crib with an infant or toddler.
   k. *Limit* the number of toys and keep large toys *out.*
7. *Vaporizers* and *humidifiers:* Keep them away from cribs and play areas. *Watch cords. Never* point at child.
8. *Toys: Keep up* with consumer safety regulations; in general:
   a. Watch for cheaply made rattles that can easily open and that have small parts that can easily be swallowed.
   b. *Stuffed toys* should be tightly furred and have sewn-on features rather than small plastic pieces that can be mouthed off. *Remove* neck ribbons. *Check* for wires.

c. *Play yard gyms* and *mobiles* should be *removed* as soon as the child can pull self up. All should have secured and nontoxic pieces.
d. *Watch* light and inexpensive *riding toys.* Make sure that riding toys are low enough, sturdy enough, and secure enough so the child will not cause the toy to be top heavy and fall over.
e. Make sure toys are *age appropriate. Remove* small pieces until you are sure that child is ready for them. *Observe* first use of new toys in supervised conditions.
f. Make sure all toys are *nontoxic.* Young children are very mouth-oriented, and sooner or later the toy will be there.

9. *High chairs, carriages, carriers: Never leave child unattended! Never leave child unsecured by strap! Do not* use carriers as car seats or depend on their handle to carry child's weight.
10. *Car seats:* Use only *Approved* car seats. Use only in approved manner. *Do not* allow child to get out during travel. *Do not* hold child while traveling.
11. *Diaper pails and potty chairs:* Because each container holds water, each has the potential for drowning or getting a nosy child's head caught. Use the same precautions as you would for tubs, pools, and toilets. Also, watch the pleasant smelling and attractively colored diaper pail deodorizers; they are potentially dangerous.

A few tips in general:

1. Look around in stores to catch up on safety standards *before* buying a secondhand product. Check consumer reports. Check with the U.S. Product Safety Commission. New safety standards went into effect in 1974, but many unsafe baby products are still available.
2. Paint with *no-lead paint* whenever refreshing children's equipment. *Never allow* children to be present when painting and wait until all paint is thoroughly dry before allowing children to return. *Use high-quality enamel paint.*
3. *Remember: A lack of supervision and misuse of equipment often lead to avoidable misfortune.*

TOY SAFETY AND THE YOUNG CHILD

Toys are the tools of learning for young children. Toys are the way young children manipulate and try out the mechanisms of the adult world around them. All toys should be safe, but some are not. Reasons for the existence of unsafe toys include poor workmanship, inappropriate use by younger children, poor design, lack of supervision on a toy requiring supervision, or a broken toy.

Parent's Magazine keeps parents and teachers informed about which toys are not safe. In general, remove all broken toys until you fix them or throw them out!

You also need to remove toys for younger children as children outgrow them. What is safe for an infant can be deadly to the toddler or older child. In reverse, do not allow children to use and play with toys that are for older children; the parts may be too small or dangerous for them.

Children should be taught to use any new toy they receive. Toys should be picked up by the child (with help, if needed) after playing so they do not create a safety hazard. Limiting the number of toys left out on any one day is an easy way to lessen the task of picking up a multitude of toys, which can seem overwhelming to the child. The fringe benefits of limiting toys are that the child feels less bored and the stored toys are like new friends when its their turn to be put out.

Good toys for your child often do not include what is advertised on television. Many heavily promoted toys are the least likely to last and most likely to bore the child. Ask yourself the following questions *before* purchasing a toy:

1. Is it age (developmentally) appropriate?
2. Does it have any sharp edges, small parts to break off easily?
3. Does it require small batteries that a young child might easily swallow?
4. Does it do everything, or does it allow for input and interaction with the children and their imagination?

Outdoor Play Equipment

Outdoor play equipment also needs to be checked periodically. Make sure screws are covered, swings are grounded or cemented, and rusty spots are repainted; keep bikes in top order; and keep the play area clear and safe.

OUTDOOR PLAYGROUND SAFETY RULES

1. *Keep equipment in good repair.* Missing screws or bolts, chipping paint, unsecured equipment, and makeshift repairs are all potential dangers to the children using the equipment.
2. *Make sure equipment is developmentally appropriate.* As children grow, their play equipment needs to become more challenging for their skill development. Young children need to be told that an inappropriate piece of equipment for them is *off limits* until they reach a certain age or attain a certain level of skill.

3. *Always supervise properly.* Young children should *never* be left alone in a play area. Climbing equipment needs to have on-the-spot supervision; if a child attempting a new skill is in trouble, an adult is present to help and reinforce while keeping the child from harm.
4. *Choose sturdy, well-built play equipment.* Although an inexpensive piece of equipment may seem a good buy, invariably the better made piece ends up being the better value because of lower maintenance costs, longer use, and less danger to the children.
5. *Limit the number of children on certain equipment.* Some pieces are of more appeal at times, but limiting use to two or three children allows you a better supervisory position and also teaches the children sharing, how to wait for a turn, and that you are concerned about their safety.
6. *Have boundaries clearly marked for play areas.* Ball playing may be done in an area delineated by cones, away from swings and riding toys. Tell the children what to do if the ball strays out of the allowed area; for example, to stop and call the teacher or mom. Fencing may be necessary, but often you can use a tree or other existing marker to show the children the boundaries. If fencing is used, be sure each fence is at least four feet high and secure.
7. *Riding toys* should be ridden on a flat or paved area to be used most safely. It is recommended that you have a STOP sign where you want the children to stop, especially if approaching a sidewalk or street. Traffic tickets can be given out the first few days until the children learn to stop at the sign. A third reminder to stop on a given day means loss of driving privilege for the remainder of the day while you lead the offender to another activity. The worst offender soon learns to follow the "STOP sign" rule, and this rule eliminates the need for constant reminding and nagging. Broken toys as always should be in the repair shop and *Never* in use.
8. *Ball playing should be limited and restricted* to use of soft or safe balls. Young children should not have hard balls of any type. Foam balls are excellent; rubber inflated balls are also fine. The potential for tragedy or harm is great when a young ball player kicks, hits, or is hit by a hard ball. For the same reason, wooden or metal bats should not be used.
9. *Sand-box play* is a great activity for young children. All children should be taught these safety rules *before* using the box.
   a. *No throwing sand.*
   b. *No removing sand from the box.*
   c. *Do not use metal trucks with sharp corners.*

   Discussion should follow the statement of each rule as to the danger if the rule is not heeded. Again, *strictly enforce* all safety rules. A *cover* for the sandbox is also a good idea to prevent neighborhood cats from leaving unsavory deposits that could be harmful to children. Old shower curtains with elastic around the edge or stapled to wood slats or plywood make good, inexpensive covers.

10. *Sticks* and *stones* are very much a part of the outdoor environment. Sticks make wonderful pencils for writing in sand. Most children have rock collections at one time or another. However, unsupervised use and abuse of sticks and stones offers the possibility of harm. Therefore, prohibit the use of both sticks and stones except during special times when the children are closely supervised and are working on a project. This is especially important when you have several children in the yard. I have rarely seen children play with sticks when play did not eventually disintegrate into potentially dangerous sword play.
11. *Climbers* are great, but they should *Never* be placed on tar or cement. They need a soft and obstacle-free surface on which the potential climber can safely fall. Limit the number of climbers. Climbers must wear crepe- or rubber-soled shoes. Leather slips.
12. *Slides* need to be used carefully. Railings are a must, particularly at the top. The height of the slide should be age appropriate. A twelve-foot slide is very high for preschoolers. A wide and lower slide is safer for young ones. Climbing up the slide and sliding head-first should not be allowed. Also, keep the area at the bottom soft and free of obstructions, including other children.
13. *Swing sets* should be cemented into the ground for maximum security. Bolts should be secure, with sharp edges covered. Leather or belt-type swings should be used; the potential for concussion is higher with heavy wooden swings. Jumping off swings and walking in front of or behind swings should *never* be allowed. Some *Toddler swings* are not safe; they can tip. Check the consumer guides before you buy or ask people with toddlers which swings have been safe for them.

COMMON-SENSE SAFETY RULES FOR THE PRESCHOOL AND DAY-CARE CENTER

1. *Limit* the number of children for activities. For example, allow only two at the water table at a time and three at the swing set. These limitations promote better safety and less chance of accident.
2. *Carpentry area:* Start out with only a hammer and nails. Limit use to two children. Make sure the children wear safety glasses. Add screwdriver and screws, then the hand drill, and finally the saw as the children learn to use the tools appropriately and safely. Immediately remove any child who after one warning does not follow safety rules. The carpentry area is a wonderful learning experience, but it can be dangerous and must be especially well watched, with all rules strictly enforced.

Beware of pressure-treated wood as it contains arsenic. Do not allow pieces of this wood to be used in the carpentry area at all. It can be very hazardous to children, especially when sanding. If in doubt about a piece of wood, check with a local lumberyard about the wood's safety factor. Treated wood is often greenish in color.

3. *Classroom set-up:* Set up the room so you have busy areas such as carpentry and art near each other and quiet areas such as reading and puzzles near each other. *Keep total visibility* of the whole room at all times. Do not use high barriers to separate your interest areas. Keep easily tipped furniture securely attached to the floor so that an accidental tipping is impossible.
   a. Be sure drapes or curtains are fireproof and about six inches above any heating baseboards or outlets.
   b. Be sure hot radiators are covered to prevent accidental burns.
   c. Be sure that your water play area is away from any electrical outlets.
   d. Do *not* use powdered paints, prepackaged papier mache, permanent markers, or crazy glues with young children. These are on the banned list for use with young children. Their use over a period of time can cause lung and neurological problems.
   e. Purchase safe chairs that do not tip easily when little ones are using them. A good chair is heavier at the base and has firm legs.
   f. *Lofts* are terrific play areas but require extra supervision. There should be a secure railing for climbing up to the top and around the loft itself. If the railing has slats, be sure they are so close together that a hand or head will not get stuck between the slats, causing an accidental death. Place a rug underneath a loft in case of a fall. For young children, the loft should be no higher than four feet off the ground.
   g. *Electrical outlets:* As previously recommended, use clear outlet covers. Be sure that outlets are ample. It is less expensive to have an electrician add a few extra outlets than to replace a school damaged by a fire caused by overloaded outlets.
   h. *Keep heavy objects* on the floor; never place them on bookcases or above the children's head level when they are sitting on the floor.
   i. *Second-hand equipment:* Watch out for it. Such equipment can save money, *but* always check the current market and safety lists before buying. Some older equipment and furniture is *not safe* for children's use at all or without alterations. The person selling second-hand materials and toys probably would not know about needed changes. *Be a wary shopper.*
   j. *Gym equipment:* Do not use a trampoline with young children unless you are properly trained in its use, have adequate adult spotters, and follow all safety standards. If you use inner tubes for part of your program, be sure that the tube plug is covered well with tapes and padding. The tube plug can cause a nasty cut if left uncovered. In general, be cer-

tain that any and all equipment is properly secured before use and that the teachers using the equipment are properly trained in all safety concerns.

4. *Hanging objects:* Most preschools and day-care centers hang pictures, mobiles, and other objects from the ceilings. Be careful that anything you hang is lightweight and high enough up to eliminate the temptation to pull or hang oneself.
5. *Step stools:* Stools that you and/or the children use should be bottom heavy and wide-legged enough to be safe. Some children's stools are too narrow and tip easily.

GOOD SPORTS SENSE FOR THE YOUNG ATHLETE

More young children are getting involved in athletics and organized sports at younger ages, even in preschools and kindergartens. Whether a child is ready for organized and competitive sports is a source of controversy. Hopefully, a parent has a good sense of each child and will make any decision based on that child's needs, desires, and ability. Sports for the young child include hockey, ice skating, baseball or T-ball, competetive dance, and gymnastics. Some questions to consider *before* allowing your child to participate in sports include the following:

1. Is the child really ready physically and emotionally?
2. Has your pediatrician advised in favor of the participation? Is your child in good health?
3. Are you ready to allow the child to leave the activity if it is too much for the child?
4. Is the child self-motivated to practice?
5. How well does the child prepare for the sport? Does the child do appropriate warm-up exercises to avoid pulled muscles and torn ligaments that can keep a child from participating in sports as a young adolescent or adult?
6. Does the child have proper safety equipment and wear it always? (knee pads and lacings, for example)
7. Does your child still have time to just play or is the scheduling too ambitious?
8. Who will be teaching your child the sport? Are they knowledgeable in first aid and injury? Are they knowledgeable in the development of young children?
9. Do all the children get to play or only the select few who are better than the others? Is your team an elimination and tournament-geared team rather than one that provides sport direction and learning and competition?

10. Is your child better at individual sports that allow self-competition than at group sports in which he or she may be compared to others? Being compared to other children is always a negative feedback to the child. It often damages a child's developing sense of self and abilities. It also turns the child off to the sport or can cause the child to take foolish risks to win approval. These risks can end in permanent injury.

The sports *least* recommended for young children include:

Football
Boxing
Baseball
Tennis
Basketball
Gymnastics

These sports are not recommended because they have higher ratio of damage for the young developing body. They require coordination skills beyond most young children's normal development level. Most eliminate the clumsy, awkward, or slower child from active participation, and these are children who would most often benefit from physical activity. Also, young children should be mastering the developmental physical activities of climbing, running, balancing, jumping, throwing, and catching. These sports require a certain competency at these skills before playing that may not be present developmentally.

The sports *most* recommended for young children include:

Swimming
Skill development soccer
A well-organized gymnastics program with trained personnel

These sports tend to teach important movement skills, provide all-around fitness, have low injury rates, and can be enjoyed equally by all body types and both sexes.

QUESTIONS FOR REVIEW

1. Why is safety in the home such an important aspect of safety training for the young child?
2. With the widespread use of safety caps, why should we be concerned about children being poisoned?
3. Who is Mr. Yuk?
4. What can happen to a young child who is given alcohol?
5. What is the first thing a child should do if there is a fire?
6. Why is a prearranged meeting place in the event of a fire important for the young child?
7. What do you do if you are on fire?
8. Describe a good way to practice what to do if you are on fire.
9. What is the difference between a kitchen stove and a wood-burning stove with regard to safety and the young child?
10. When you smell gas, you should switch on the light and check the cellar. True or false?
11. What is the primary rule about children and water safety?
12. How should a child be taught to save another child who needs help in the water?
13. How do you get out of ice if you fall through?
14. Name three safety rules for children and adults to observe near water.
15. Which is safer to use with a young child in a supervised activity: a sharp or dull knife?
16. What is the rule of thumb about plant safety?
17. Name four poisonous plants.
18. What should be kept on hand for emergencies involving poisons?
19. What are the causes of lead poisoning?
20. What is the test for possible lead poisoning?
21. Who is at most risk of lead poisoning and why?
22. Why are the signs of lead poisoning so misleading?

CHAPTER 5

Street Smarts

All parents' fears begin the day their child walks alone to play with a friend. The friend may live only a couple of houses down the street—not a far distance physically, but quite a distance psychologically for a parent. The child needs to know many things to walk safely out in the world.

Street smarts can be divided into two basic areas—traffic safety and stranger safety. Traffic safety deals with cars, walking and crossing streets, and safety in the car. Stranger safety deals with recognition of a stranger; what to do if approached by a stranger on the street, in a car, and in a store; how to handle food offers by people; and how to get help if lost.

TRAFFIC SAFETY

This chapter begins with traffic safety. Every teacher and parent covers the basics with children. You need to start when children are young and to reinforce the safety aspects at every opportunity.

Automobile clubs have posters and materials that can help people teach street safety with cars. American Automobile Association (AAA) has a series of four well-designed booklets, *Preschool Children in Traffic,* for use with children aged three to six. The series also contains a parent booklet that completely explains the program. This program has a high interest factor with the children and a built-in reward because they can keep the booklets as they finish them. This also increases reinforcement because they reread the booklets at home with their parents. The content is flexible enough to use with two-year-olds to even seven- or eight-year-olds as a review.

The basic concepts about traffic safety that a young child needs to know include:

1. Cars and trucks are bigger than you are; they can hurt you.
2. Cars and trucks *cannot* stop immediately.
3. *Never* run in the street; you might fall.
4. *Never* enter the street between parked cars; walk until you can cross with *full vision.*
5. Look both ways *two times* before crossing.
6. *Wait* if a car is coming; *do not* try to beat the car.
7. *Walk facing* traffic, on the edge of the street if there is no sidewalk.
8. *Do not ride toys* in the street. Use a driveway.
9. Cross at crosswalks or street corners whenever possible.
10. Do *not* chase balls or toys into the street. Get an adult. Toys can be replaced; *you cannot!*
11. *Buckle up* in a car when you are a passenger. Wearing seat belts is now the law in many states and it saves children's lives! Buckle up the baby, too! *Never hold a child on your lap!*
12. Drivers need to watch and concentrate on traffic. Never make a lot of noise or grab when you are in a car. Never throw things at a car.
13. It is *smart* to use good traffic sense.
14. Red says STOP, green says GO, and yellow says WAIT on the traffic signal.

Children can learn all these skills and facts with fun and through games. Make a cardboard game board that looks like a street intersection complete with crosswalks and a traffic light. Using toy cars, it is easy to let each child have a turn being the driver. Using small toy people, the children can take turns being the pedestrians. Through these toys, you can role play all kinds of situations that test the children's skill. Let them see how a child gets hit by going out into the street without looking and then reinforce how awful that would be. Children like to play the Safety Game on their own, so leave it where it can be used.

Another good game to use is the driveway or sidewalk as a model of the street. Make a crosswalk across the sidewalk with white tempera (washable) paint or chalk. Make a traffic signal out of a box and a pole. Make a stop sign to show where the cars should stop so the children do not go into the street. Now, using a small riding toy as a car, the children and teacher can practice the safety rules about crossing streets. The children can also practice on their own during outdoor play. The painted crosswalk lasts a few months unless it rains a lot.

Even two-year-olds can enjoy learning the street safety rules when allowed to act out the rules during playtime. It is a realistic situation to have a crosswalk with riding toys as cars. The same safety rules about waiting at the crosswalk

Dramatizing safety at the crosswalk using riding toys is the best way to reinforce talks. A fun way to make the crosswalk is to draw the outline and let the children color it in with chalk.

until the cars pass, walking across the street, and walking bikes across the street apply to the playground riding area. Using the safety rules keeps playground injuries down while reinforcing the same behaviors for the real traffic situations. The teacher should praise the children when they obey the safety rules. Positive reinforcement from adults is always a good idea.

Taking neighborhood walks to a store or around the block is a good way to reinforce the learned concepts in the real world. Try not to tell the children what to do. Try to remind them that they have to do something at each point. Make sure that you are in the front of the line so an overanxious child does not get to the street alone. Using songs and fingerplays is fun and a source of reinforcement. Making toy cars, safety traffic lights, and learning about police officers are good extension activities for this content area. Also, Figure 5.3 contains a song called "Red on Top" to help the children learn about traffic lights.

Young children should be taught to walk bicycles across streets as part of traffic safety training.

Street smarts vary at different times of the year. In winter, wearing white at night is not always smart in the northern states because the child will blend in with the snow; in other seasons, wearing white at night makes you more visible. Inexpensive stickers that glow in the dark are terrific additions to children's sneakers, boots, and a raincoat because they show up immediately when hit with auto lights, even at dusk or on grey days. Joggers often wear them. Children's bicycles used in the street should get the glow treatment for the same reason. In the spring and fall, northern streets are apt to have a light frost in the morning or evening. Children should be extra careful when walking and crossing streets. Also in the fall, children should be careful of slippery wet leaves, which can lead to a nasty fall as they cross the street. Playing in wet leaves or leaf piles in the roadsides can also be dangerous because drivers cannot see the child in the leaves.

Even two-year-olds can be taught to wait at a crosswalk until walkers pass by. Acting it out with adult praise makes it fun to learn good safety habits.

Halloween is a fun celebration for children in most areas. However, it can be a dangerous holiday without proper planning. If your children are out trick-or-treating, they should observe these rules of safety:

1. Wear short costumes that eliminate tripping.
2. *Don't* let little ones wear *masks!* They restrict vision.
3. *Never* allow candles or matches to be used. Use flashlights or glow sticks.

4. *Never* allow young children to go trick-or-treating alone, even for a short distance. An adult should be with them. Although it is a holiday, some adults see it as a perfect opportunity to snatch or harm a child.
5. *Follow all the street safety rules.*
6. Go only to homes that are well lit and hospitable.
7. Allow *no* goodies to be eaten at all until you have checked them at home.
8. Go out *early.* Young children are quite content to go out at dusk. It is dark enough.
9. *Limit* the length of your route. Young ones get tired easily.

A traffic safety certificate can be given out at the end of this content area.

STRANGER SAFETY

Stranger safety, the other aspect of street smarts, is not as easy to teach as traffic safety. Remember your parents' admonishments when you were a child about needing to behave for elders. As a child, you were supposed to obey your elders, respect them, and be polite. It was rude not to respond when spoken to by an adult. It is difficult to reconcile this kind of upbringing with the need to protect children from strangers. Most people want well-behaved children. It is possible to have both well-behaved and aware children, but it takes some changes in our own thinking about expectations as far as politeness in children. A parent may gulp when a daughter refuses to answer that nice old man who just asked her her name and told her how pretty she was, but this is only a momentary embarrassment and it may someday save her life.

Let us first look at how a child perceives a stranger. Adults have the discretion and experience to size up a situation and a person; children have neither the age nor experience to do this accurately. Adults might decide to give directions to a person in a car from a safe distance if the person looks all right, the child might get too close to the car or not be able to tell if the person looks all right. The child could get grabbed easily if unaware. If the person went by the house everyday and waved, the child probably would perceive this person as a friend and *not* as a stranger even though the child had never met the person. A child can meet a person when with parents and then perceive this person as a friend because the parent introduced them. The person may have been a mere casual acquaintance, but it is unlikely the child will see the relationship this way. Adults working with children do not want to frighten children every time they meet a new person, but children need help to learn the difference between someone they meet and a trusted adult. *Turtle Magazine* has good features about child safety. An excellent poem addresses this problem using the character Turtle.

TURTLE KNOWS
Turtle doesn't talk to strangers,
No matter how friendly they are.
He won't take anything from them
Or get in a stranger's car.

Most strangers are just nice people
That you simply haven't met
But, sad to say, there are others
Who are bad and a dangerous threat.

Better to be safe than sorry,
Is a saying that's old but true,
So Turtle won't take any chances
and wants YOU to be careful too![1]

Notice that the poem reinforces a good attitude toward most people while warning about the bad. The best way to handle this teaching is to role play and talk about what could happen and what are the child's alternatives. Get the children to tell you their options. Starting with the ridiculous helps the ball get rolling and sets up the discussion to get beyond simplistic answers.

Example

What does a stranger look like?

Is he ten feet tall and green?

Is she covered with blue fur like Cookie Monster?

Can a stranger be a giant?

Next, ask more serious questions:

Example

Can a stranger look regular?

Can a woman be a stranger?

Can older people be strangers?

---

1. Poem by Betty Winn Fuller. From TURTLE MAGAZINE FOR PRESCHOOL KIDS, copyright © 1984 by Benjamin Franklin Literary & Medical Society, Inc., Indianapolis, Indiana. Reprinted by permission of the publisher.

FIGURE 5.1
Strangers.

Always allow time for the children to think over each question and to respond with their own ideas. Accept the child's ideas; if they are wrong, *gently* direct them into rethinking until the sense of the situation comes to them. This can take time. The adult needs to help the children come to a clear understanding that every person they meet is not trusted like a parent.

Now that the children have an understanding of who can be a stranger, they need to work out situations and solutions to situations. Here are some role plays that should be tried with the children.

Example

1. You are walking home. A car stops and the woman offers you a ride home because it started raining. You should ____________________
2. You are walking to Jeremy's house and a man smiles and starts walking with you. You should ____________________
3. A car is following you as you walk with your friend. You should ____________________
4. As you walk by an alley, someone grabs out at you. You should ____________________
5. You are in the store when a person follows you around. You should ____________________
6. A man who looks very nice stops his truck by your house and asks you if you would like to take a ride to see his other trucks. You can drive too! You should ____________________
7. A sweet lady stops her car and asks if you would like to see her new puppy. Come closer because he'll run away if I let him out there. You should ____________________
8. A nice looking older man stops his car to ask directions. You should ____________________

These role plays and others point out to you, the adult, the range of situations a child could encounter. The child who has role played and discussed what to do or say in these situations will have a better chance to handle the situation safely. The basic stranger safety rules are still intact. Never take a ride in a car with anyone. We are adding that the child should not even go near the car. If a car stops near the child or is following the child, that child should turn in the opposite direction and go back to the house from which he or she came or to the nearest safe house. (A safe house is one you have told the children ahead of time is allowed for them to go to in an emergency.) If the person goes to get out of the car, the child should scream and run. If someone calls the child to their car to see something or take a ride, never go near the car. Children do not have to answer strangers just because they are adults.

Children have to be detectives. They have to understand that some people are sneaky and some people lie just to get a child to come to the car. Tell the children: Don't be fooled! Be smart detectives! If you really want to see what a stranger has to show, run home and ask mom or dad first. Ask them to come see it with you. I bet if it's that good, they'd want to see it too!

Some strangers are so sneaky that they might try to tell you that your mom is hurt and she sent them to get you. Don't believe it! If mom is hurt, she'd send only one of the special people to get you or the person coming would know your family password. A good detective is not fooled by a person who does not know the password. Don't get near the person! Special people are people you tell the children are allowed to pick them up anytime mom or dad cannot be there. Most nursery schools require parents to state in writing who has permission to pick up the child. Special adults are people whom you trust.

The password (codeword) is a special and easy-to-remember word or phrase that identifies a person as safe to the children. In other words, this person is safe to go with. Why might a family need a password? An adult might not be able to pick up the children or arrange transportation with one of the people designated as a special person. The adult thus needs a way to let the children know that a certain person is authorized to pick them up. Knowing a password also empowers the children to test a stranger who tries to talk them into coming.

The password should be a family secret. Even when preschoolers try to tell their safety trainer their password, gently tell them that it must be kept a secret for their family. A teacher cannot even tell the children her family password! Some good ideas to use for passwords are baby names, an old nickname, or a favorite toy's name. You want to pick a very easy-to-remember name and practice it with the child.

(When my daughter was at a little league game, the level of her understanding about the importance of the password was made clear to me. My brother stopped by and asked to pick up my daughter and bring her out for supper. I gave him the password because this was a sudden change of plans and I could not let her know. My brother, a favorite uncle, forgot the password. My daughter refused to leave with him; she called home from the snack house to check if I had cleared the supper trip. My brother was embarrassed, but I was thrilled. If she was this careful with her uncle, I felt that she would remember to be careful with anyone.)

Another reason to keep the password secret is that people who kidnap or abuse children are often known to the child. By using the password, *only* the

Make a Traffic Light:

1. Cut circles.
2. Paste on rectangle in arrangement of lights.
3. Staple or glue onto craft-stick.

Make a large light for play-yard.
Alternative: Make various street signs, such as: STOP.

Detective Glass:

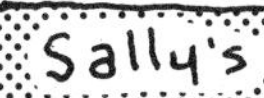

1. Cut two pieces of oaktag or cardboard into above shape with center hole.
2. Glue plastic wrap to one piece of cardboard for magnifying glass.
3. Glue on top of other cardboard.

Detective Hat:

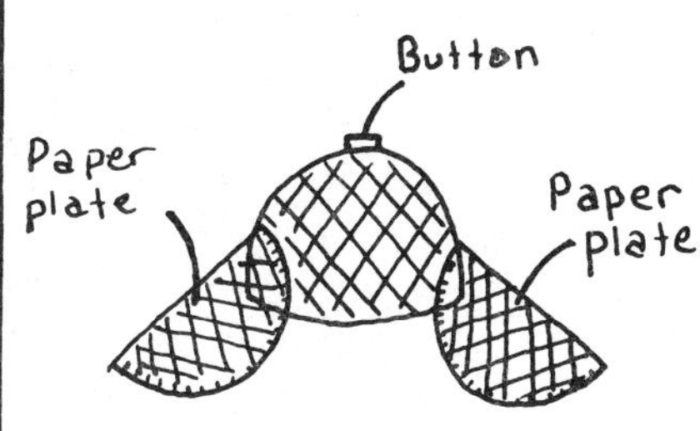

1. Color two plates and one paper bowl.
2. Add crisscross stripes in black for plaid.
3. Staple or glue plates and bowl together.
4. Glue button on top.

FIGURE 5.2
Three safety games to make with the children.

person an adult knows and sends will be able to take the child. This method may not be foolproof, but it is worth the effort.

One of the most difficult ideas for children to understand is that anyone can be a stranger. You do not want a child to be fearful of all adults or bigger children. Children need to be able to trust people, but they also need to be cautious. This is plain, good, common sense.

If we want to encourage the children's right to be tuned in to their gut feelings of danger, then we have to allow them the right to make noise and a scene if they feel threatened. Most times, this step would not be necessary, but the option should be discussed and it should be the child's. Making a scene is difficult for many adults to accept because they were taught *never* to make a scene in a public place.

People who have dealt with the cases of molesters and/or kidnappers (other than professionals), such as police and psychologists, say that often the victimizer attempts to make an initial contact. When making this initial contact, they are assuming they will encounter a scared, frightened, and quiet child. A child who responds by making a noisy scene is likely to be left alone while the victimizer leaves quickly to avoid notice. You can empower children to bite, kick, give the safety yell, and scream, *"This is not my mother (father)"* if someone tries to grab them or begins to follow them in a store or mall. Many adults ignore children yelling in stores. You may even have felt sorry for the mother of a screaming child. But what if the adult were *not* the mother?

Children should be told to go to the nearest store clerk and tell her or him that a stranger is following them or a person is being bothersome. Under no circumstances should the child leave the store until the clerk has located you or the store has called you in case the stranger is waiting outside. Many stores and malls have security guards or police officers. These are two other people your children should be told are safe to approach if they are bothered.

You need to practice the "What-if" game until your children or classes are comfortable and sound more confident with their responses. Be positive with the children and supportive. Listening to the children and giving them permission to act will enhance the likelihood that they will act accordingly in a real situation. Use car rides to reinforce role plays with children. Playing car games can reduce the usual sibling fighting, and the children get good at the game. In fact, the older ones often make up situations themselves. Understand that this method does not advocate rude children; manners are important. Children can still be polite to other people. When children are with parents, expect them to be courteous and polite to all people encountered. When they are alone, however, you do not want them to answer, speak with, or go near anyone no matter what is said to them. The same is true for cars. *Stay away.* This is easy enough to help the child understand. Ask the children if adults are lost, do they ask children for help? The answer is no. Adults do not ask three-year-olds for directions or help. Adults seek out other adults for help. An extenuating circumstance could change that, and as the children get older in their teens things will change. In the meanwhile, I think this is a fair evaluation of most adult-child relationships.

At a recent talk to a men's group about safety training and children, a nice older gentlemen expressed sadness at children's being trained not to talk to nice strangers such as himself. He expressed the pleasure it gave him to speak with little ones because his grandchildren lived far away. I asked him what he wanted children to experience when he spoke with them. He replied only that they smile if he said how nice they looked. I asked him why he had to ask the child's name to pay a compliment. I also asked how he would feel if his grandchild were there and someone she did not know tried to ask her name. We agreed that older people could compliment a child and see the smile and yet leave the child's safety training intact by not trying for a response or asking for a name. Other adults need to see the sense in how we are trying to teach young children so they can also help.

Telephone Safety

Chapter 4 mentions that telephone safety and at the door at home safety will be discussed here. These topics are best discussed after the password concept.

Young children are often intimidated by telephone calls. They think they have to respond and adults tell them not to hang up the telephone as we run to answer a call. No wonder they answer the voice on the phone. When a child is home and the telephone rings, the child should answer the phone politely. If an adult is not home, have the child learn to say, "Please call back. Mom is in the shower." Then the child should say goodbye and hang up immediately. This procedure is polite and safe. If someone were casing your house or child, they have received no information of worth and do not know if an adult is present. With young children, you would rather know they were safe and miss a few telephone calls than have them at risk. Children are an easy target for the telemarketing people who are trained to sound like a friend; they often have some personal information. These types of telephone calls can confuse the child. Being told to hang up after a two-line polite answer will lessen the confusion. Tell the children at the preschool, "You have the right to hang up the telephone anytime you feel funny about the call or if it scares you."

Figure 5.3 includes a song on telephone safety to sing with the children.

Door Safety

Strangers at the door can be another danger for children. They love to open doors and say hello. This practice can be dangerous whether you live in an apartment or single home. Again, the child's perceptions of strangers are important.

Red to top

Red on top	*(point up)*
Green below	*(point down)*
Red says, STOP,	*(hold out palm)*
Green says, GO.	*(motion to move)*
Yellow says, WAIT	*(wag finger side to side)*
Even if you're late.	*(wag finger side to side)*

Telephone Song
(sung to: *ABC Song*)

743 7982 *(substitute each child's own telephone number)*
That's what I'm supposed to do
743, yes, dial it true,
Now the 7982
I am fine, how are you?

675, now I've begun,
1761, now I'm done,
675 1761
Let's play outdoors in the sun,
675 1761
Come to my house, we'll have fun.
by Mildred Hoffman, Tacoma, Washington

I am a Policeman
(sung to: *I'm a Little Teapot*)

I am a policeman, with my star,
I help people near and far
If you have a problem, call on me
I will be there, 1, 2, 3.
by Judy Hall, Wytheville, Virginia

FIGURE 5.3
More safety songs. ("Telephone Song" and "I Am a Policeman" from More Piggyback Songs, *compiled by Jean Warren. Everett, Wash.: Totline Press, Warren Publishing House. Used with permission.)*

Children will open a door to a stranger if they do not perceive the person as a stranger. A person who walks by every day, a delivery or garbage truck driver they see on a regular basis, almost any casual person could be perceived as a friend. Therefore, to say that the child should not open the door to a stranger will not necessarily keep strangers out.

Some people are very clever at scaring or tricking children into opening the door. Again, the need to be a superduper snooper detective must be stressed. Tell children that no matter what anyone says at the door, *do not open it!* Try some role plays and practice them. Let the children play detective and figure out the answers.

Example

Does the person at the door know the password?

If mom was hurt, what did she say she would do?

Did mom or dad say someone was expected?

If I'm frightened, do I have to answer the door?

If not, what could I do?

The person at the door is in uniform and says I have to sign for something; is it a present? What do I do?

Many children and adults are duped by that kind of person at the door. Most delivery companies are reputable. Adults should call and verify with the company before opening the door. Children should be told to tell the delivery person to leave the package or bring it tomorrow and never to open the door. The parent can then check to be sure it is a real delivery. Of course, if the parent is home, the child can say wait and run to get the parent before opening the door. Even if a uniformed officer comes to the door, the door should not be opened until an adult calls to check.

THE POLICE

Learning about street smarts should include a visit to a police station or a visit from a police officer. (Call your local police station to arrange this.) The children are often confused about their feelings for police officers. So often, television incorrectly shows police as gun happy and frightening to children. Some children run and hide under furniture when a police officer walks into the classroom. If we are going to tell children that this is a person they can turn to for help, we have to change perceptions toward the police.

It was a real shock for our preschoolers when we visited Officer Willie at our local police station. Officer Willie was terrific with the children. He showed them his uniform, badge, and even his gun, explaining everything as he went.

The children were so surprised when he told them he had never fired his gun except on a practice range and never unholstered it unless he was going to use it. He typed name tags for each child and fingerprinted the children. The children loved it. He showed the children how emergency calls come in and even let them talk to different officers who were out on patrol.

When we returned to class, we set up our police station with an old manual typewriter, microphone, a switchboard, and our uniforms. The children had a great time playing. When coupled with our ministreet in the schoolyard, the experience was more realistic than the police experiences television often portrays. Figure 5.3 contains a policeman song that the children can learn.

AUTOMOBILE SAFETY

Another aspect of safety that the police emphasize with young children is auto safety. The children are asked if they buckle up with their seat belts. In Massachusetts, New York, California, and some other states seat belt use for children under the age of five is mandatory. Children are especially vulnerable to being injured in accidents. Their small bodies make excellent projectiles on impact. Some people still allow their children to stand up in the front seat or lie across the back window. These behaviors and holding an infant or toddler in an adult's arms can be deadly to the child. On impact, the adult's body will fall forward and can crush the child against the dash. Deaths have been attributed to this practice. Adults who care about children teach them the sense in buckling up and make sure that they do.

Some good, free brochures are available from AAA (American Automobile Association, Traffic Safety Department, Falls Church, Virginia 22047). They explain the statistics and need for buckling up. They can be sent home to parents in the preschool program or day-care center every year as a gentle reminder. Many preschools allow children to go on trips only in cars with seat belts for every child. The AAA also has a series of excellent posters available at no cost. These posters illustrate the safety rules of walking and driving for children and are designed by children. There are National Safety Council materials that are super and usually available free. Buckle Up Bear Coloring Book is another good way to reinforce seat belt safety.

Adults also should discuss cars and how big they are. Take the children on a walk around a car that has been driven into the school yard.

Example
Ask: How big are the tires next to you?

Can you lift the car?

Is it hard or soft?

After a grand inspection, talk about how difficult it is for a car to stop immediately because it is so big and heavy. Talk about how a child could get hurt because the car is so heavy and hard. This helps them see the sense in following good street safety. It is a good idea to let each child sit in the driver's seat and look out the rear mirror to see if he or she can see another child behind the car. A common reason for accidents involving small children is that drivers do not see them behind the vehicle. This test really proves it to the child. It reinforces the safety rule about walking between or behind parked cars.

POINTS TO PONDER ABOUT STRANGER DANGER

Young children often feel that if someone knows their name, the person is all right and must know them. Therefore, tell your children in school and at home that just because someone calls their name does not mean the person is safe; in fact, that person should be treated as if a stranger. Play a game of how could that person learn my name:

1. Heard a friend call me.
2. Read my name on a barrette, school bag, socks, etc.
3. Heard mom call me.
4. Saw it on the mailbox.
5. Read it on the apartment buzzer.
6. Guessed it.

This game serves to increase awareness for children and make them less vulnerable.

Danger to children could come from someone known to you. Never tell children to do everything a person says. Leave them some discretion to say "No" if threatened. Children are much brighter than many people credit. At an early age, they know the difference between a danger situation and being a little wise guy. Rarely do children take advantage of this discretionary power.

Do not leave children unattended in a car, store, or at home. Many children have been kidnapped out from under the noses of their parents who only ran in the store for just a minute. Kidnapping only takes a minute. It seems a burden to take several children in the store for a short time, but it is worth it.

For emergencies, set up several telephone friends for your children. These people include a retired or shut in neighbor or someone whom you know is home a lot and can trust. This practice gives a child someone to call if they are unsure of what to do if you are not home, or if something happened to you and they panic. Switch off with a friend as telephone friend for older children if they are sitting alone. Have a retired neighbor as an emergency telephone friend for the younger ones. The children love it. It makes them feel safe and they can establish a friendship with an elderly person or couple.

Teach your children the *Buddy system.* Children should never go anywhere without a buddy or friend. If they are shopping, or in a restaurant, two go together to the bathroom. If a child wants to walk to the pond to fish, get a buddy to go. Even if a child wants to ride a bike, get a buddy to go. Again, remember that most molesters and kidnappers want to find a single child; numbers alone can help prevent an initial attempt at a child. This is no guarantee, but it can make a difference, especially when the system is started young and reinforced so that children go and come together without splitting up.

Know your child's routes to school, to friends' homes and other spots they frequent. Know who their friends are. Know where you are letting them go when you give permission for visits. Tell them they cannot visit a friend unless you know or have met the parent, and never can they visit unless the parent is home. No overnight visits are permitted unless you know the parents well. This practice will not make you popular with the children, but it can work out for the best.

Each morning, note what your children are wearing. In case you need to look for a lost child, you need to know what he or she had on.

Knowing Telephone Numbers

Children should be taught their telephone number as soon as possible. A song can help. Once the children learn their telephone number, add area code and teach them how to make a long distance collect call. It may make the difference between a forever lost child and a child who can come home. Few kidnappers stay where they take a child. If your child can dial home from another state, your child can reach you. From kindergarten on, give your children an emergency quarter taped into a school bag or sewn into their coat pocket so they can always call home in an emergency.

Learning to dial "0" is a task even a two-year-old can use to summon help. The older child can be taught to dial 911 or your local town emergency number for help in an emergency. Keep emergency and friends' numbers posted by the telephone.

Knowing Addresses

Children should learn their street address. Then add town or city, state, and country as the child is ready. This is an added protection. Do you know how many Main Streets there are in the United States? Do you know how many states have a Falmouth or a Millbury? A street address is not enough. A good time to practice the address is at night before bed. You can practice before evening prayers or bed time story.

Move on to the next content area. Don't forget to put the sticker on the chart.

TIPS FOR CHILDREN WHEN WALKING

1. If you are being followed, turn into the nearest safe house and knock. If you are not near a house, go into a store, shop, or public building and ask for help. A good person to approach is a mother with children.
2. If you are being followed by a car, turn and go back where you were coming from. The car has to go up and turn around.
3. If you are approaching a person or group of people who make you feel uncomfortable, cross the street. Always walk confidently and do not appear to be preoccupied.
4. Walk on sidewalks. Walk as close to the side of the road as possible when there are no sidewalks, and always walk facing traffic.
5. Walk with a buddy whenever possible.
6. Make sure your parents or caregiver know where you are going.
7. Avoid alleys and dark or secluded areas. Take the long way near houses. Shortcuts are not always the best way to go, especially early in the morning or at dusk.
8. Do not talk to strangers.
9. Cross on the crosswalk whenever possible. Cross at corners.
10. Follow the safety rules for crossing streets by listening and looking for traffic.
11. Be alert for cars that do not slow down or stop.
12. Never run into the street for any toy or object. Always ask an adult first.
13. School groups should travel with the buddy system. Holding a rope is a good trick to use with small children so they all stay together on busy streets or in malls. The rope is usually about five or six feet long. Another good technique for groups is to put brightly colored pinnies on the children so they all match and are easy to spot if any children break away from the group. Red, yellow, orange, and lime green are excellent colors for quick visibility. Large or extra large T-shirts can also serve instead of pinnies, although the cost is a little higher.

QUESTIONS FOR REVIEW

1. What is included in the packet *Preschool Children in Traffic*?
2. Name six basic concepts of traffic safety.
3. Name one of the three traffic safety reinforcement activities cited in the chapter.
4. What is the difference in how an adult perceives a stranger and a child perceives a stranger?
5. Should a child answer a driver of a vehicle who stops to talk?
6. What is a safe house?
7. A password or codeword is used ________________________________.
8. What makes a good codeword?
9. When should you encourage children to make a scene in a public place?
10. What should children yell if they feel threatened or are grabbed?
11. To whom should a child turn for help?
12. What is a child's right in regard to the telephone?
13. Role plays are very important to reinforce concepts about opening doors to strangers. What are some of the ruses clever people use to get people to open the door?
14. What can be learned from a visit to the police station?
15. What are the dangers of not using seat belts in cars for the preschooler and young child?
16. Name some seasonal considerations about street safety for children.
17. What should you tell children about people who know their names?
18. What is a telephone friend?
19. Explain the buddy system.
20. Once children know their telephone number, the next step is ________

    ____.
21. In what detail should you teach young children their address?
22. Name two tips for children when walking.

CHAPTER 6

Victimization Prevention

Children are victimized by peers, older children, and adults. Sometimes a bully takes a snack at nursery school; sometimes it is a sexual assault.

Why are some children victimized and some seem to avoid it? What makes a difference? Is it some lucky trait or twist of fate? Sometimes the child is unable to prevent or stop the situation because the child does not know how. No one is born knowing how to handle social situations. We all are taught either through words or actions of people around us how to behave. Children are physically smaller than adults. Children are dependent on adults and need to trust adults in order to survive. Children have to do as they are told and can be forced to by the bigger and more powerful adult. For these reasons, children make easy victims.

Our society has stereotypes about children that reinforce people seeing them as victims. Some of the images discussed at the Children's Awareness Training (CAT)[1] included innocent, helpless, impulsive, mouthy, imaginative, story tellers, objects to be taught, vacuums to be filled, not aware, and images of either devil or angel naughty or good. These myths about children make it easy for a victimizer to try to convince people that the child lied, misunderstood, or made up a story. You know how children are.

1. The Children's Awareness Training (CAT) was designed by the Worcester (Mass.) Rape Crisis Center in conjunction with Camp Fire Girls and the Massachusetts Department of Mental Health.

CHILDREN'S RIGHTS

Children have rights. They have the same right to be respected and believed as do adults. We recognize that color, creed, and sex are not valid reasons to stereotype or act in a prejudicial manner. We recognize that various adult groups have rights. The time has come to recognize children's rights and teach the children these rights.

Two strategies involved in the Children's Awareness Training are important groundwork in helping children understand their rights. "Strategy: To change the social position of children as powerless.

A. To help children realize and define their personal rights.
B. To help children recognize actions which threaten or violate those rights.
C. To equip children with skills to prevent or deal with the violation of the rights.

Stratgegy: To reduce children's isolation.

A. To establish support networks for children among their peers. . . .
C. To increase awareness among children and adults of existing community resources."[2]

FIVE SENSES

The first step in teaching children is to make them aware of the senses. Young children are learning body sense awareness of their *five basic senses:* sight, hearing, smell, touch, and taste. The children enjoy learning how these senses work. Tasting parties in which children are blindfolded and try to guess what food they are tasting is a fun way to learn about taste. There are many good games for learning the five senses.

For the purposes of beginning to develop a sense of a child's rights, we take this learning of the senses one step further. The end of this chapter contains a sample of a senses booklet the children make themselves. Once children have learned the five basic senses, which is a usual part of any preschool program through games, puzzles, and hands-on experience, ask them to make a special booklet all about their senses. They can draw, color, or write something they like or dislike about each sense.

---

2. Central Massachusetts Camp Fire and Worcester Area Rape Crisis Program and Worcester Area Mental Health, *Children's Awareness Training* (Worcester, Mass., supported by Federal Grant R 18 MH 37549-01, 1982, 1983, 1984), 9.

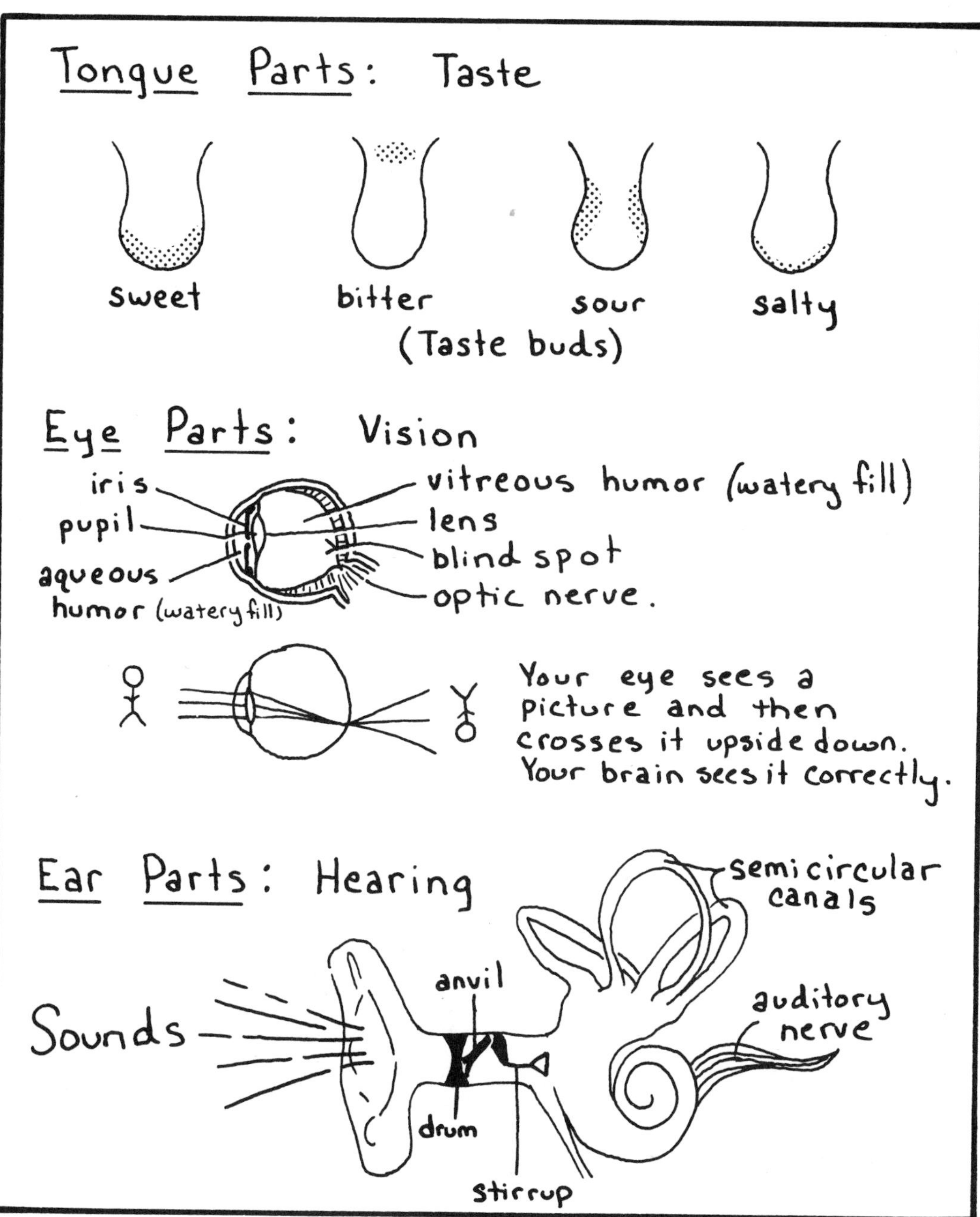

FIGURE 6.1
Taste, vision, and hearing.

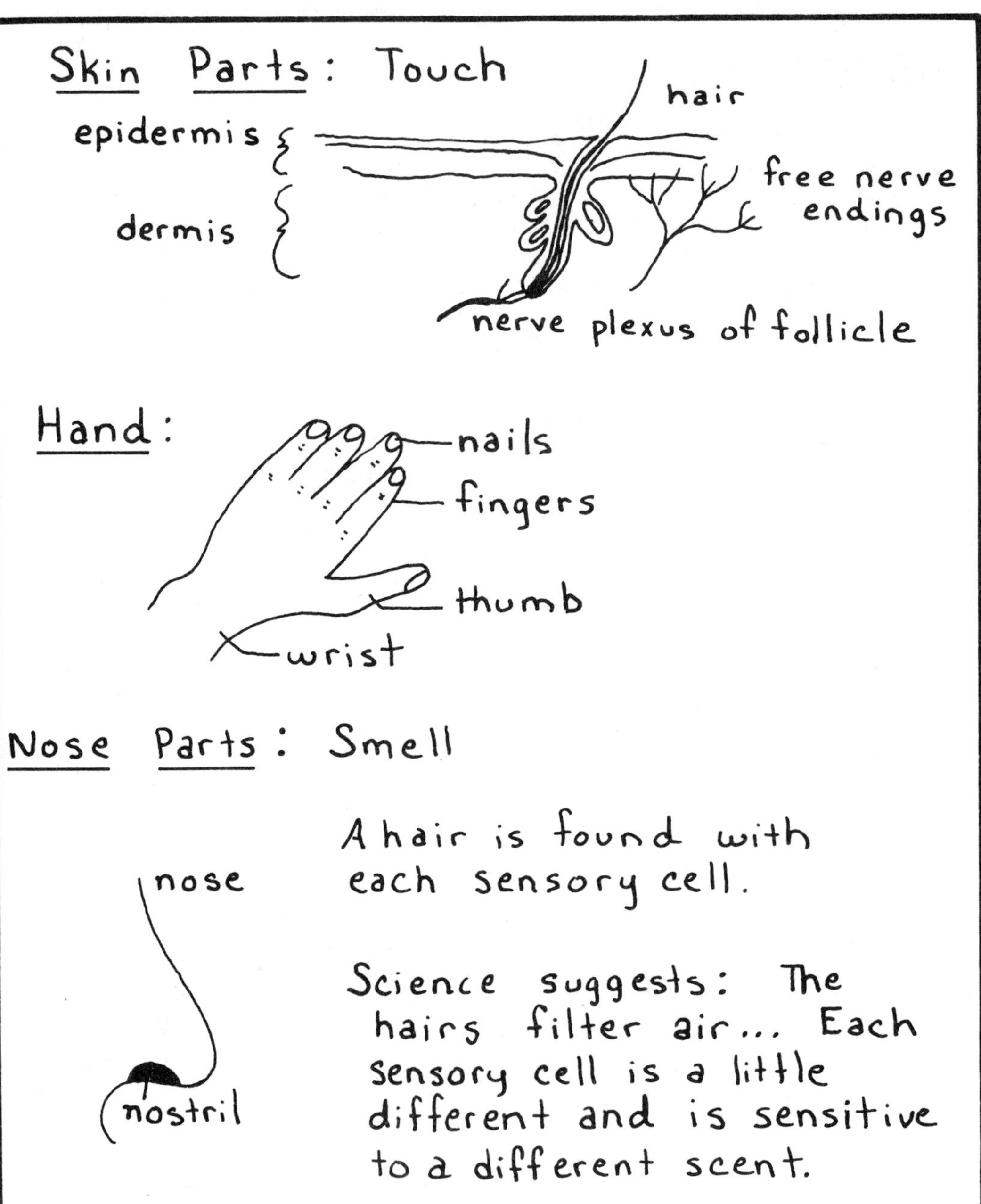

FIGURE 6.2
Touch and smell.

Vision

Play "Blindman's Bluff"
Play "Pin the Tail on the Donkey"
Go on a Vision Walk. When you come back, draw as many things as you can remember seeing.

Smell

Cover eyes and try to guess what something is by its scent.
Try putting an apple slice under the nose while an onion slice is in the room. See what happens.
Point out scents: cooking apple sauce.

Scent bottles: put coffee and spices in jars. Punch holes in tops of jars. See if children can guess contents by scent. Make cards to coordinate. Put jar on correct card (cinnamon, onion, extracts on cotton balls).

Touch

Use a "feely box" or a tin can covered with a sock. Put objects in and try to guess what each is by feeling it.
Foot paint with tempera paint, soap. How does it feel?
Touch various textures and describe them. For example: shaving cream, sand paper, velvet, etc.
Fingerpaint with pudding, jello, or shaving cream.

Mr. Touch

FIGURE 6.3
Vision, smell, and touch activities.

Hearing

Tape home sounds. Let the children guess each.
Tape school sounds, traffic sounds and other sounds.
Take a listening walk. Have children tell you the sound as they hear it; then all listen for the sound.
Play four or five sounds at once and have children listen for one sound. For example, use a drum, a cymbal, a triangle, tapping sticks and a horn, or use household items such as a blender, a washing machine, and the like.

As you learn about each sound, talk about how we need to care for our special senses.

Eyes – Not straining, not looking at the sun, and not putting anything near our eyes.

Ears – Not playing loud music or noises. Not putting things in our ears such as cotton swabs, etc.

Nose – Not putting things in our nose unless a Doctor tells us to.

Tongue – No sharp things in the mouth. No very hot things in the mouth.

Hands and Body's Skin – Be careful of hot and sharp objects. Be careful not to bang your body around. Treat your body as a friend.

FIGURE 6.4
Hearing activities and general special senses tips.

Fun with the Five Senses

Cover example

Make a Sense Book.

With my ears I hear...
(draw things you can hear or cut and paste things you can hear.)

With my eyes I see...
(draw things you can see or cut and paste things you can see.)

With my nose I smell...
Have a smelling game. Then have the children color and paste a picture of each thing they could smell.

With my hands I feel...
Have the children cut various textures: corduroy, velvet, vinyl, etc.

With my tongue I can taste...
After learning the 4 basic taste buds (① Sour, ② Bitter, ③ Sweet, ④ Salt), have a tasting party. Then have the children paste the powder they tasted on the correct part of the tongue.

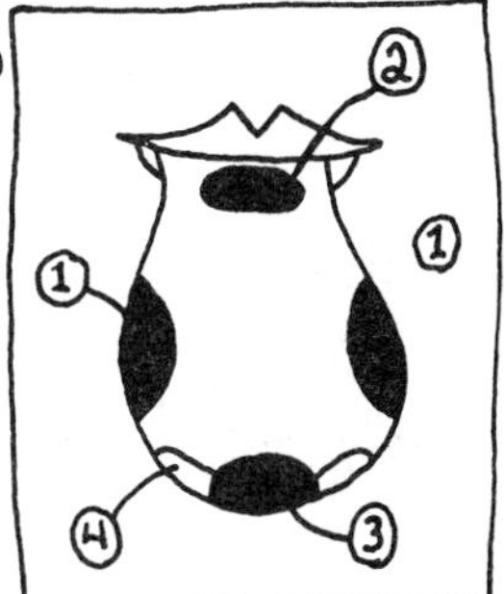

* Use salt, alum, sugar, and onion powder for tasting.

FIGURE 6.5
Fun with the five senses.

MY BOOK ABOUT SENSES

by ____________

With my eyes I hate to see...

With my eyes I like to see...

With my ears I like to hear...

FIGURE 6.6
Senses booklet.

With my ears I hate to hear...	With my nose I like to smell...
With my nose I hate to smell...	With my mouth I like to taste...

Senses booklet.

With my mouth I hate to taste...	With my hands I like to feel...
With my hands I hate to feel...	I like the warm fuzzy feeling when...

Senses booklet.

I didn't like the feeling when...

I got a funny feeling when...

These pages should be larger, at least 8" x 11" each, for younger children. You should do only one page or set of senses at a time. Let the child color in any colors. Talk about the subject to be drawn first. The conversation is more important than the drawing itself with the young child. The drawing serves to validate your feeling that the child's thoughts are important. The book also allows the opportunity to review or to use it to help the child communicate a problem to the adult.

Senses booklet.

Example

With my ears I like to hear . . .

With my hands I hate to feel . . .

This is a first step to validating the feelings that we all have in relation to our senses. This process can take days or can be done quickly, depending on the age and inclination of the children. The activities can be more physical; but the concept is to get the feelings toward each sense in booklet form. Talking about each page as it is completed further encourages the development of the feelings concept and the right to have these feelings.

Other Senses

After discussing the five senses, it is time to talk about other senses. We all have a special sense. It's that "funny feeling" in your stomach when something just is not quite right. Ask the children if there is a time they can remember when they had a funny feeling, when they felt uncomfortable.

The other feeling sense we all have is the warm fuzzy or security feeling, which is the opposite of the funny feeling. It is the feeling when we feel warm and loved and good about ourselves. Continue the discussion about this feeling. Ask the children when they felt this way. Now finish the feeling booklets with these last two emotions.

Personal Space

The next step is to build on the concept established earlier about personal space or Spiderman senses. Remember, personal space is the invisible line around us that sets off the funny feeling if it is violated or crossed.

Exercise: Personal Space

Have the children divide into pairs and stand at arm's length from each other. Slowly move closer to each other until one person says, 'Stop, I feel uncomfortable.' (That person has just invaded her/his personal space)"[3] Talk about and review how it felt and who can and cannot come into the space. Follow this with a drawing of people I feel good about coming into my space and people I do not really want in my personal space.

3. Central Mass. Camp Fire et al., 29.

Bullies

The next step is to have the child learn about a bully. A bully is anyone who violates your personal space or tries to take away your rights. (A list of children's rights is at the end of this chapter.) When role playing from this point on, follow these guidelines because role plays of rights violations can be upsetting for some children.

"In each of these situations, freeze the scene at the point the child does not know how to respond, or shows anxiety, or the offender would be successful.

- Ask the child how they felt. Compare those feelings to being safe, strong and free. Focus on any funny feeling or warning signals. Acknowledge and support any feelings of fear.
- Emphasize that the offender has no right to do what he did, that he was to blame, *not the child.*
- Ask children what could have been done differently. Focus on realistic and strong responses. Fantasy or avoidance responses should be acknowledged as such while supporting the child who volunteered the suggestion.
- Focus on assertiveness, peer support and telling a trusted adult.
- Redo the situation using these suggestions. . . .
- Do not allow children to play the part of the offender. This would be reinforcing offender behavior.
- All role playing is optional. Children should not be pressured to participate."[4]

Now is the time to do some role plays about bullies. Try to think of typical situations to which young children can easily relate. Some situations could be the following:

Examples

The little boy up the street comes into the yard to play. He grabs your toy that you were using. You try to take it back but he yells at you and threatens to punch you.

You and Joe are sharing a bag of chips. A bigger boy comes along and grabs the bag.

Sally has a new doll. Diane comes up and asks to see the doll. Diane tells Sally she wants the doll. Sally tells Diane that it's a new doll. Diane stands up very close and says, "Give me the doll now." Sally sadly hands the doll over and Diane walks off with the doll.

---

4. Central Mass. Camp Fire et al., 30.

In all these situations, you want to make a point: "When someone takes away our rights, we have problems." In general, children have three rights—to be safe, strong, and free. You should talk with the children about when they feel safe, what it means to be strong, and what it means to be free. As you finish the discussion of each situation, ask the children if they felt safe, strong, and free. Why or why not? What could be done to change the situation?

Brainstorm prevention strategies. Ask the group how the 'victim child' could have kept her rights. . . . Focus on strong, positive responses: standing up to the bully, asking another group member to help, or telling an adult."[5] Now go back and redo the situation and plug in the new solutions. The role plays should end successfully for the child. Some children may need help in saying NO to a bully. I know that sounds incredible to those who listen to the average young child saying "No, no, no" all day. Remember, this type of situation is not one in which the child is dealing with a nice, safe adult. Often, children meekly give in because they feel forced or intimidated. Playing the NO game can help all young children. "Saying NO Game—Take turns with someone; ask a favor of each other—just pretending. Let the answer always be no. Try saying 'No' in different ways. Help each other to say it firmly, like you mean it. 'Thank you for asking me but the answer is no.' 'No I don't feel like it.'"[6] Jack Hagenbuch, Jr., regulation administrator of Massachusetts Society for the Prevention of Cruelty to Children, says problems involving abuse of children, particularly sexual abuse, can very often be avoided if the child says, NO! When asked why they abused one child and left a sibling alone, abusers answered, "The other child said NO, and she'd tell her mother." Remember also that we have to reteach ourselves as adults to accept children's right to say NO and validate their right to accept their feeling of uncomfortableness. If Uncle Gus wants a kiss and the child feels uncomfortable about this, do not pressure the child to give Uncle Gus a kiss. It is the child's right not to. Handshakes can be just as friendly and they avoid a violation of the child's rights.

Tattling versus Telling

Sometimes a person who violates children's rights threatens them with harm if they tell. Sometimes a person who violates children's rights tells them it is a secret. Children need to understand the difference between tattling and telling.

This is confusing for children, because we tell them not to be tattletales. The story sheet at the end of this chapter clearly indicates the difference between tattling and telling. Use the sheet as a springboard for discussion. Talk about the two little girls, Tattling Terra and Telling Tillie, and elicit from the

5. Central Mass. Camp Fire et al., 32.

6. Jennifer Fay, *He Told Me Not to Tell* (King County Rape Relief, 305 S. 43rd, Renton, Wash., 98055, copyright 1979), 15. Used with permission.

Once I was a Tattling Terra when...	
Once I was a Telling Tillie when...	
Tattling Terra...  tells to get others in trouble! tells to show off! tells to get attention!	Telling Tillie... tells to help someone! tells to help herself! tells because it is right to tell some things! 
can use Tattling Tom...	can use Telling Tim...

FIGURE 6.7
Telling versus tattling handout.

Good Secrets

get told make people happy
make you feel good

Some good secrets are birthday presents or parties.

Once I had a good secret...

Bad Secrets

never can be told
make people scared or unhappy
make you feel unhappy or bad

Some bad secrets might be lying or cheating

Other bad secrets might be...

BAD SECRETS NEED TO BE TOLD!

FIGURE 6.8
Good secrets and bad secrets handout.

children the times each one has played both roles. Then talk about how it is *not tattling* to talk with a trusted adult or a parent. Secrets are brought up at this point. Often, a child will not tell about an abusive or threatening situation because they made a secret promise not to tell. Children need to learn the difference between a good secret and a bad secret. Use the story sheet on secrets for a discussion starter and a follow-up take home sheet. Even very young children are sharp enough to learn and remember the difference.

SEXUAL VICTIMIZATION

Sexual victimization is another area of concern children need to know how to deal with. I realize that this subject goes against most of society's sense of right. It would be remiss, however, not to complete the children's safety training by including this necessary information just because the thought disturbs our sensitivities. It is difficult to think that someone who you know and trust could commit this type of crime, but it can and does happen. The adage "forewarned is forearmed" is still true.

What kind of force could a person use to make a child agree to an act of sexual victimization?

"The force may involve:

- taking advantage of someone who is younger . . . .
- bribery
  'I'll let you watch T.V. till midnight if you. . . .'
- threats of:
  harm to the child . . . .
  harm to the offender
    'If you tell, I'll go to jail'
  withdrawal of affection
    'I won't like you anymore'
  break-up of family
    'This would really hurt your mom.'
- taking advantage of the child's lack of knowledge and dependency on adults
  'It's OK, everybody does it'
  'I'm just checking you out, now that you're getting older.'
  'What's the matter, don't you like me?'

From an adult's point of view, these coercive statements may not seem forceful. To the child, they are."[7]

---

7. Jennifer Fay, *He Told Me Not to Tell* (King County Rape Relief, 305 S.43rd, Renton, Wash. 98055, copyright 1979), 6. Used with permission.

Wait a minute. This material may seem to you to be too frightening for a preschooler or a young child. But you are wrong. Far better the child learns naturally while learning other protective skills such as traffic safety and home safety from a caring adult than experience the betrayal of adult trust and victimization because the child did not know what was going on.

Statistics

The sexual victimization rate of children is currently set at one out of three or four; one out of three children will be sexually victimized before reaching eighteen years old—girls and boys. Most people who molest children do not fit our long-time idea of a molester. In "75 percent[8] of all sexual abuse cases, the child is assaulted by an adult she or he knows and trusts: a family member, a neighbor, a babysitter, a relative, a family friend. Most parents fear assault of their children by a stranger and therefore only prepare children for this possibility . . . . Sexual abuse affects families from all socio-economic classes . . . . Many offenders are upstanding community citizens . . . [who] can not be easily distinguished from others . . . . They won't be recognized in the grocery store, the classroom or behind the pulpit . . . . Child molesters and incest offenders seek their own gratification at the expense of children. Their feelings of importance stem from the exploitation of those weaker and less powerful than they. . . . Children already know about sexual assault from watching television, movies and the radio . . . . sad is that the information children lack is 1. how to protect themselves . . . . 2. what to do and who to tell . . . . 3. how to recognize it . . . . Children choose who they want to be affectionate with based on their trust of the adult. This does not change because children learn that someone they know and trust may try to touch them in an inappropriate way. It simply gives them the right and the skills to stop that type of touch. Children who have control over their bodies and control over how and by whom their bodies can be touched will be comfortable returning truly affectionate behavior."[9]

Knowledge will not turn your child into a scared and cold child. Children properly trained in sexual victimization prevention will not display any problems, fears, or lack of affection for parents. In fact, the feedback has been very positive that the children will feel stronger and better about themselves. Talking about real situations often reveals that the children have thought of them and have had many misconceptions that were worse than learning the truth and that were relieved by discussions. What age should children be when you start talking about and preparing them in victim prevention? Two years old is a good age to begin preparing your child for victimization prevention.

---

8. Many professionals involved in child abuse situations feel that it is as high as 95 percent for the young child.

9. Central Mass. Camp Fire et al., 3–4.

Touch

Let's address the subject of touch. Touch is a part of all human beings' lives. It starts the moment you are born. Your mother hugged you; it felt good and warm and safe. Babies are fondled and cuddled; they need this touch to thrive and develop. As we grow, touch stays an essential part of our life. We learn there are touches we like and others we do not like.

In talking to children, you can call the good touches *warm fuzzies* or *green light feelings*. The confusing touches are called *yellow light feelings* (for children who are four or five years old and older). The bad touches are called *red light feelings* (include yellow light feelings with red for younger children). Using the traffic signal lights builds on the concept children have learned and are comfortable using. They already understand that red means STOP, yellow means CAUTION, and green means GO. The next step is to extend the color coding to include feelings. If children know that red means STOP, it is easy for them to remember that red light feelings must mean STOP and TELL. the worksheet-take-home sheet in this chapter shows the three feelings. Having the children brainstorm and talk about these feelings is a good way to begin this discussion. The children can draw or write each type of feeling that may have happened to them in the appropriate box. Remember, if you are using the sheet with younger children (ages two to four years old), you may want to adapt it so only a green and red light are showing and make the spot lights larger. The confusing touch will be the most difficult for the children to understand. It can be a hug that is too hard or a tickle that doesn't feel right or a touch that feels good and bad at the same time. If children are not sure about a touch, they can ask these questions:

Example

". . . who? Do I want this person to touch me?

what? Do I want this type of touch?

when? Do I want to be touched right now?

where? Do I want to be touched in this place?

why? Why is this person touching me? . . . do I feel safe, strong and free?"[10]

When learning about touch, it is important for children to know the exact names for their private parts. Basically, private parts are those that are covered by a bathing suit. The private parts should be labeled with their real names and not by cute or family names; chest or breasts, vulva, penis, anus, and gluteus maximus (behind). Children should use these names at school and at home.

10. Central Mass. Camp Fire et al., 41.

Green Light Feelings

are wonderful!

can be funny, sad, happy -
but are good!

Red Light Feelings

can be confusing, upsetting.
can be bad feelings that:

Need to be shared with an adult.
Need to be talked about.

Sometimes they are half good and half bad.

RED LIGHT FEELINGS NEED TO BE TALKED ABOUT

(for use with children under five years of age)

FIGURE 6.9
Green light and red light feelings handout for young children.

Green Light Feelings

are terrific!
can be happy, sad or funny!
make you feel good inside-warm!
can be snuggles, hugs,
handshakes, etc!
are not upsetting or confusing!
make you feel safe!

*Yellow Light Feelings

can be O.K. but you're not sure!
make you feel funny inside!
can be confused-mixed up feelings!
can start O.K., but then not be!
need to be talked about!

*Red Light Feelings

can be upsetting!
can hurt!
make you feel scared or not safe!
or angry or upset or bad!

* NEED TO BE TOLD RIGHT AWAY! *

NEED TO BE SHARED WITH AN ADULT–

a trusted adult!

priest/minister/rabbi/teacher/
parent/nurse/doctor/coach/favorite
aunt or friend/etc.

(for use with children over five years of age)

FIGURE 6.10
Green light, yellow light, and red light feelings handout for older children.

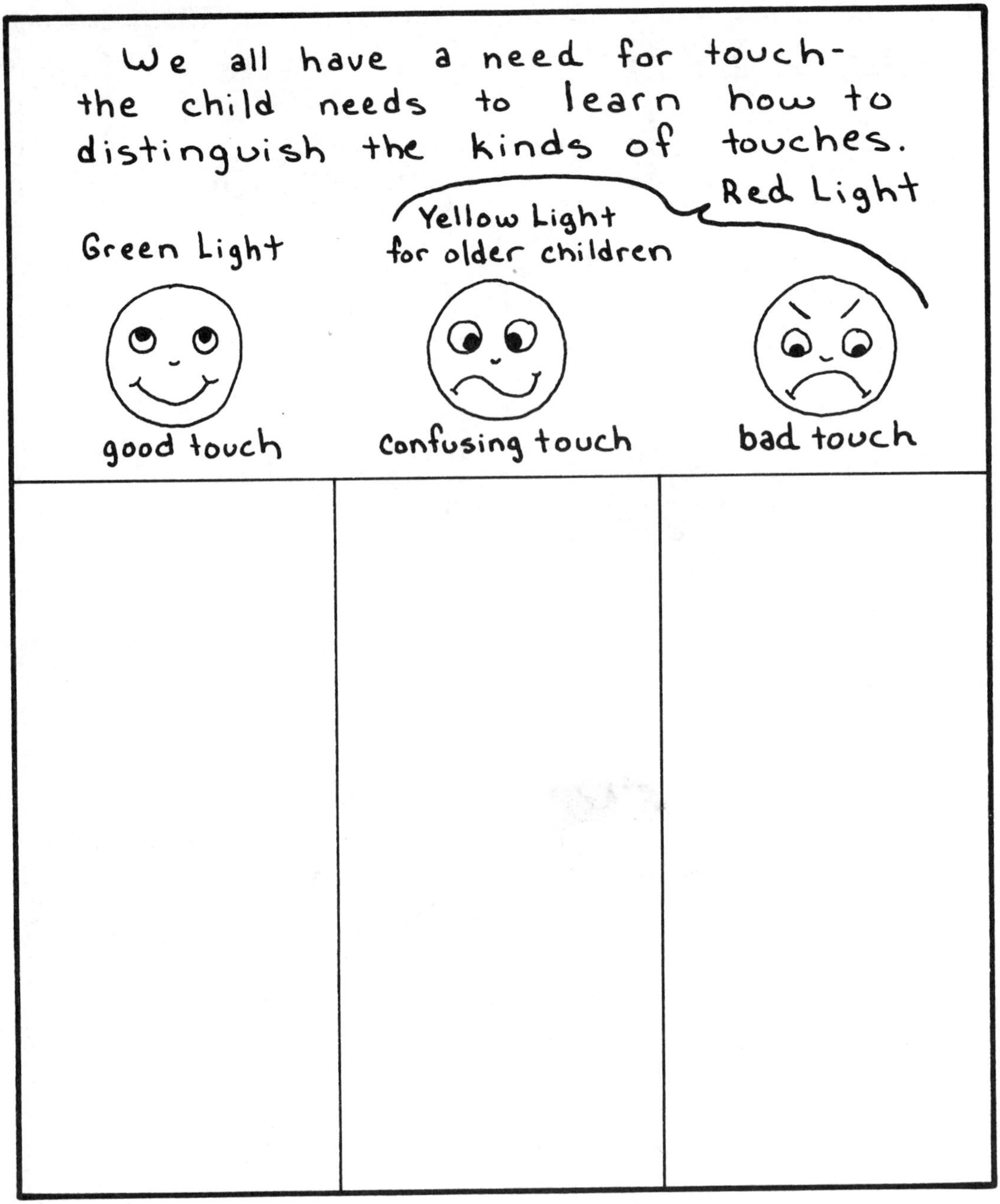

We all have a need for touch- the child needs to learn how to distinguish the kinds of touches.

Green Light

Yellow Light for older children

Red Light

good touch

confusing touch

bad touch

FIGURE 6.11
Good touch, confusing touch, bad touch handouts.

We all have a need for touch. The child needs to learn how to distinguish the kinds of touches. Have child draw or write a time he or she had a...

color me GREEN	good touch - green light
color me YELLOW *	confusing touch - *(yellow) red light
color me RED	bad touch - red light

Good touch, confusing touch, bad touch handouts.

That is why a take-home sheet such as Figure 6-12 is an important link with the parent(s). It clearly informs them of what information you are teaching at school and what procedures you are telling their children to follow. Home and school cooperation are very instrumental in the success of the program.

Common sense must again be brought in when you discuss with young children the issue of touching. Of course, there are appropriate times when a young child will need to be touched in private areas. Two-year-olds are toilet training and often need help from a parent, sitter, or teacher. Every young child needs help in the tub or shower. A doctor or nurse surely checks a child in private areas during a physical exam. The children need to understand that at these times touching is not a bad or red light situation.

What the children need to understand, and can if presented calmly and matter-of-factly, is that if anyone touches their private parts at other times when help is not needed, then they have the right to say no and tell. A loud NO is most appropriate.

Telling the parents, teacher, or another trusted adult is the second and equally important part of this safety strategy. The children also need to understand that if someone does not stop when they say no, it's alright. They still should do the second part, which is to tell. Always reinforce the concepts that it is not the children's fault that the incident occurred, and that you will not be angry with them even if saying no did not stop the touching.

When children are confused about a touch, they have the right to ask questions. A person who is touching a child in a manner that causes confusion is taking away the child's rights to feel safe, strong, and free. "In addition, it is helpful for children to know the proper names for their genitalia. This teaches them respect for their bodies . . . If children don't know the proper names . . . they may have a hard time describing what happened to them if they became victims some day. Many police officers sadly note the embarrassment of the child who only knows terms like 'whiffie' or 'cucumber.' The child wants others to know what happened but is limited by an enigmatic, cutesy vocabulary."[11] Also it makes it difficult for a child to explain to an adult a confusing problem. The poor vocabulary might keep children from preventing a bad touch situation because the adult they tried to explain it to might not understand.

A good time to teach the child the correct terminology is when you teach body parts, and do it as normally and low key as you would toes or hand or any other body part names. This way the child is comfortable using the names. Tub time is an easy time to slip in terminology by saying such normal sentences as, "Be sure you wash your ears and your penis (or vagina)," or "Oops, you forgot to wash your chest." It is helpful for the child to teach the correct body part names from the beginning for all the body parts. I know from experience that it is much harder for children to unlearn those funny little nicknames and

---

11. Linda Tschirhart Sanford, *Come Tell Me Right Away* (Fayetteville, N.Y.: Ed-U Press, 1980), 19.

What and Where are my Private Parts?

Parts covered by my bathing suit are my Private Parts. I need to learn the right words for my private parts.

Private parts are: gluteus maximus (tush, behind, bum)
chest or breasts (girl)
vulva (girl)
penis (boy)
anus (both)

Can anyone touch these parts? I can.
Mom, Dad or someone else like a babysitter or teacher if they are helping me with: shower, tub, or toilet.
- Doctors and nurses when they check me.

Can anyone just touch these parts because they want to with no reason or permission?

NO!

what can I do? Say **NO!** real loud!
Tell Mom/Dad/Teacher or trusted adult!

YELL **NO!** AND TELL!

FIGURE 6.12
Private parts and touching.

CHILD SAFETY TRAINING and YOUR CHILD

A part of our program at Becker Junior College Campus Preschool is to teach your children about themselves, their body, their world around them. Always included in the past have been school and home safety, traffic and street safety, our good health, body parts, and emotional good health.

This year, we are expanding our usual curriculum to include Stranger Danger and Sexual Victimization Prevention. Bits and pieces will be introduced throughout the year until we are ready for a more in-depth understanding. Before introducing this unit, we will hold a Parent meeting at which we will show you exactly what and how we intend to cover the subject matter with your children. Questions will be welcome then or before.

The director and head teacher are as concerned as you are about the well-being and safety of your children. Safety skills are very important for young children because they are very vulnerable. We have carefully put together what we feel is a positive and nonthreatening approach that is built on your child's feelings of strength and security. We do not want frightened children, only prepared children who through that preparation will be able to avoid being a statistic.

The statistics are frightening: one in four girls and one in six boys will be victimized before age eighteen. Since most victimization will statistically take place initially during the ages from two to six, I think that it becomes obvious that this is the age to begin safety skill development.

Your input and permission will be asked for before the sexual aspects of training. We expect to do this part of the training in January or February.

Thank you for your continued support of our program.

Sincerely,

Director

FIGURE 6.13
Sample parent initial newsletter.

relearn the correct terms when they come to school than if they learned the correct names at the outset. Knowing the proper names also helps children learn body and spatial awareness.

The children should now understand that their body belongs to themselves. They need to hear short stories of situations that are possible, followed by a talk or discussion about what the child in the story could have done to keep safe. The CAT program has an excellent story about "Uncle Harry and Amy." The story appears at the end of this chapter. You preface the story by telling the children that you have a story about a little girl and her uncle. You might feel a little embarrassed, that's all right. Then you read the story. Please change the name of the girl if you have an Amy in your room or group. After reading story, sensitively go over the points for discussion that follow the story.

You have just handled the most difficult part for adults when dealing with this topic. It was not so bad and the children were not upset when read the story. The story should end up with the affirmation that children have

the right to be safe, strong, and free.
the right to say no, even to an adult you know.
the right not to be touched in a way you don't like.
the right to get help
the right to be believed.[12]

REVIEW ACTIVITIES

You now should check whether the learnings about strangers and safety have been remembered and become part of the children's normal selves. Building on the traffic signal idea and borrowing from the traditional children's game of "Red Light, Green Light" are easy and nonverbal ways to check every child quickly and easily.

Each child makes a red light and a green light. The red light is a 6-inch paper plate colored red with a sad face on it. The green light is a 6-inch paper plate colored green with a happy face on it. You can also add a confused face on the red plate. Staple a small wooden stick on each plate so the children can raise and lower their lights as needed.

For older children, take a long rectangular piece of paper and fold it in thirds. Color each third as if it was a traffic light. Green on top, yellow in the middle, and red at the bottom (in some regions the lights may be in a different order on the traffic signals; follow your local order). Take a second piece of paper that is a little wider and shorter. Make two cuts about two inches from the top and

12. Central Mass. Camp Fire et al., 44.

Watch Out For Strangers

Watch out for strangers
Or there will be dangers.

Keep yourself at least two arms away
Or you might not see the next day.

If you see someone you don't know
Just keep on walking, don't start talking.
by Shannon Gray

Bright At Night

When you go out at night
Be sure to wear something bright.
Be sure to wear something white.
Or stay under a street light.
by Katherine Comer

Stranger Danger

Stay away from strangers.
They could be bad.
Don't talk.
Just walk.
by Shawn Lussier, Dawson Road School

Halloween Safety

Halloween safety is really lots of fun.
Just make sure you get all the rules done.
You really shouldn't run along the dark streets.
Make sure your parents check your candy before you eat.
by Joseph Nolette, Dawson Road School

Seatbelts Are For Safety

Seatbelts are for safety.
I'm glad that they are a law.
If people did not wear them,
They might not have a jaw.
by Trevor Johnson, Dawson Road School

FIGURE 6.14
Personal safety rhymes. Use children's own poetry either dictated or written to augment your safety curriculum. Older children love to share and write with younger ones. The poems make a great reinforcement tool.

Street Safety

If you are about to cross the street,
Watch out for cars,
And keep to the beat.
If you do what I say,
You'll be here another day.
by Michael Lewis, Dawson Road School

Street Smarts

If a stranger asks if you want a ride,
Please don't go with them.
Go to the other street side.
Then start to walk the other way,
You'll be safe the rest of the day.
by Katherine Comer

Drugs

Be careful of gangs and other bad guys,
They could give you a big surprise.
They could give you drugs,
And call you neat,
But I think you should know,
Drugs are no treat.
by Kristen Connolly, Dawson Road School

Stranger Danger

Stay away from those strangers
Who you don't really know.
All you have to say is NO, NO, NO,
And GO, GO, GO!
by Tyler Bradshaw, Dawson Road School

Street Safety

Always walk on the sidewalk,
Never cross at a dangerous intersection.
Don't stop in the middle of the street and talk.
Never jump, play or run,
When you're crossing sidewalk to sidewalk.
by Scott Shirey, Dawson Road School

Personal safety rhymes.

two inches from the bottom that go across but do not quite extend to the edge on either side. Slide the first paper through the two slices on the second paper. Now you can slide the paper up and down, exposing one color segment at a time in the area between the slices. The children can move their papers up and down to demonstrate that they recognize which color segment or light is needed to answer your situations in the game to follow. The children can add a happy face to green, a confused face to the yellow, and a sad face to the red area.

To play the game, the children sit in a semicircle so you can quickly assess all answers. Relate several situations to the children. They talk about whether each one is a red light feeling, green light feeling, or a yellow light feeling. When you have all decided, the children either hold up their red light signal or green light signal as appropriate or slide their traffic light to expose the correct color light. They do this about three or four times. The children then listen to a situation and either raise the appropriate light or slide their light to the color feeling that they feel is a correct response. If you see a child changing an opinion after looking at peers, then you have an inkling that this child is still unsure. *Do not say this child is right or wrong.* Ask the children why they thought red (or green) was a good choice for that situation. Talk it over, and if the child agrees, then allow him or her time to change the signal. This game takes time but it does perform well as a reinforcement for the safety situations to end with positive results. Do not rush the discussions. You may repeat and take a week or two to practice this game. Also, ask the children what they think could be done about a particular situation or what would happen if they told or said NO.

Another variation on the game is to cover three flashlights with cellophane paper—red, yellow, and green. Let three children each hold one light and turn on the appropriate light after the class decides which feeling is happening in a given situation, or let one child choose which light would be appropriate and then explain why to classmates. The rest of the class could affirm the answer or pose a problem with that response. Discussion would follow. Use of real lights is a good tool in helping the children remember.

A follow-up art activity is to make a traffic signal with three cellophane lights. The signal could be taken home with a list of situations so the parents and children could practice and discuss the situations. The child would be able to flash a personal flashlight through the cellophane, thus "lighting" the signal.

You can tell which children are unsure of their responses and can repeat whatever safety learnings you feel the child needs to build up a confidence level and safety responses. By practicing responses and recognition of a problem, the child becomes more at ease.

Some of the stories to use can include the following examples.

Examples

"A babysitter wants you to play a 'special game.' He starts to touch you in a way that feels strange.

A close friend of your dad's tries to put his hand between your legs while he's hugging you hello. Then he tells you to keep it a secret."[13]

You are at a friend's house and an adult wants to be alone with you in a room while your friend is playing in the den.

A relative asks you to come into a room at his house and then asks you to touch his penis.

A man on your street offers you a ride to get an ice cream. He tells you it will be okay and you don't have to ask mom.

You are getting a nice backrub by your cousin and then he starts to rub your bottom and near your private parts.

A bigger boy tells you that he'll teach you a new game but it has to be kept a secret because it's so special. You can't tell anyone, not even mom or dad.

VICTIMIZATION

You can see that these stories are specific and unfortunately also very possible. These stories are also good for discussion after the Uncle Harry Story for problem solving about how the child could handle each situation. Saying NO as we learned earlier comes in handy now. It also is important that the children learn to tune into the "Funny Feeling" and recognize their rights because some of these situations are subtle beginnings of victimization. For example, the back rub that slowly changes can confuse children without training; they may not be sure it is wrong even though it may suddenly make them uncomfortable. It is also a good idea to instill in the children's minds their right to remove someone's hand if it is on their body and to try a few situations in which a person pretends to touch them by accident. The child has the right to object to accidental touches. One person related that she had a relative who commented on how grown up she was getting as she began to develop breasts at an early age; he hugged her hello so tightly that her breasts were very close to his chest. She said it made her feel self-conscious and hurt but she was not sure until she was older that it was wrong of him. No other adults noticed anything wrong. This occurrence again points out the need to respect your child's judgment about family and friend hugs and kisses by not forcing the child if he or she feels "funny" about it.

13. Central Mass. Camp Fire et al., 44.

A REMINDER

VIP VIP VIP VIP VIP VIP VIP VIP

MEETING MEETING MEETING MEETING MEETING MEETING

PARENTS PARENTS PARENTS PARENTS PARENTS

VERY IMPORTANT PARENTS MEETING

TUESDAY EVENING: February 19th
WHERE: Becker Junior College Campus Preschool
TIME: 7:30 P.M.
REFRESHMENTS WILL BE SERVED

TOPIC: "Safeguarding Your Child from Sexual Victimization"

We CAN DO something to make a difference

We want you to know the What, How, and Why of our special Victimization Prevention program.

PLEASE MAKE EVERY EFFORT TO ATTEND

PLEASE remember to bring a face-view, wallet-size picture of your child to the meeting. We want to be able to do the fingerprinting with your children on Thursday. Officer Smith will be coming in then. Please return your permission slip before that class.

THANK YOU FOR YOUR CONTINUED COOPERATION! See you Tuesday!

Becker Junior College Campus Preschool From all the staff

FIGURE 6.15
Sample parent newsletter.

Self-Defense

Another way to protect the child from harm of physical or sexual assault is self-defense. But what can young children physically do to repel a possible attack? They are so small. Remember that small does not have to mean powerless. "The purpose of self-defense is to 'hurt the assaulter enough to enable you to get away.' This is not a fair fight. Remind them that this is serious business and not tricks to be used on the playground."[14]

Children gain a certain sense of power and self-confidence when they know a few simple ways to defend themselves. Children are also intelligent enough to understand that these techniques should be used *only* in an emergency and not at any other time. However, practice of the techniques is crucial so that in a real emergency, the children will feel comfortable using the techniques. The story of the boy who cried wolf is good to use at this point to establish the need *not* to fool around with these defense moves. This story helps the children realize that an abuse of the cry for help or of a defensive move will make them more vulnerable to harm.

The first defense that can easily be taught to children of most any age is the yell. The CAT program has taught an excellent yell that should become known as an international cry for help from children. The special yell is low-pitched and comes from the diaphragm. This technique enables the child to yell longer and the sound to carry farther because it causes less strain on the vocal cords. It also can startle an adult, who is used to the usual high-pitched screams most children make. An adult is more apt to notice this yell. The child can also yell, "This is not my mommy (daddy)!" or "I need help!" or some other short phrase that indicates the child is in trouble. A person shopping or passing by is much more apt to interfere on hearing this type of yell or phrase than merely on hearing a child screaming. Most often, adults feel bad for the presumed parent when they hear a child act up in a public place and are apt to ignore the normal screams. The yell itself may scare off a would be attacker because usually he or she does not want a scene and does not want to be noticed or recognized.

Children should practice the yell several times until it becomes natural. Frequent checks throughout the year also help keep the yell fresh in the children's minds. Do not forget to remind the children to use the yell only when it is needed; remind them of the wolf story. Tell the children that they can practice at home in their rooms, but only after letting their parents know that they are practicing—in other words, warn the parent that this is a drill.

Children can use two techniques to repel a would-be attacker physically. These two self-defense moves should be taught to children aged three and up. Other moves can be taught to older children. The first movement is a simple

14. Central Mass. Camp Fire et al., 35.

Children have the right to say NO when threatened. The safety yell is a special yell that is deep and carries. Practice reinforces the power of the yell and the likelihood of the child's using it in an emergency.

kick to the knee; if used immediately, it may give the child just enough time to run away. This is all we want from self-defense for the child.

This kick is especially effective if the child is grabbed from behind. The child slumps forward and then swings the heel of one foot into the knee of the attacker. Only sixteen pounds of pressure, which the child's kick could deploy,

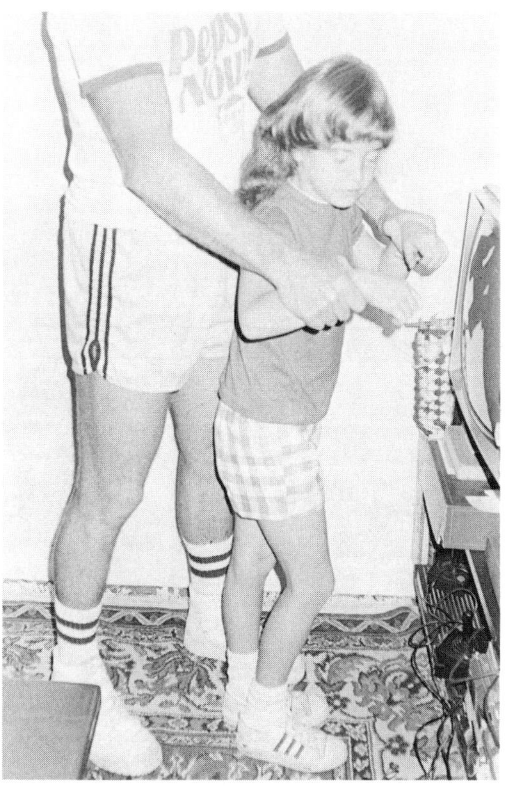

If a child is grabbed on his or her arms and cannot use move number one . . .

He or she can lift a knee while acting relaxed.

is enough to break a kneecap and cause considerable pain. If unexpected and used quickly, the kick can be enough to get the victimizer to drop his or her hands and thus allow the child to run away and yell for help. The technique must be practiced, but only with a caring and safe adult—*never with children.* When practicing, the children should not be allowed to hard kick because they could break your knee. A soft near kick is enough for practice sessions. If the child is comfortable with the technique with a trusted adult, then chances are good that the child will use it against a victimizer.

The second move is easier. The child uses his or her head for this move. The child learns to relax immediately if grabbed. The child puts his or head into a forward slump and then quickly swings it back into the solar plexis of the adult. The pressure against the solar plexis should be enough to cause the victimizer to drop his or her hands and thus give the child time to run and yell.

Basically, children have the right to do whatever they can to get out of a bad situation. These two techniques give them a few easy and physically possi-

Then, the child sharply swings the foot as hard as possible into the knee cap of the grabber. It takes relatively little pressure to break a knee cap.

At the instant the grabber releases the child, he or she runs and yells the special yell.

ble moves to help them get away. A third recommended technique is for the child to bite or lick the fingers if someone tries to put a hand over the child's mouth. Again, always stress that the idea is to get away—to yell and tell. The idea is not to stay and try to "get" the bad guy.

To whom can a child go for help? In a store or building or restaurant, the child can run to a cashier or police officer or security guard. When you are out with children, it is a good idea to point out where they could go if they were lost or in trouble. Another fairly safe and good resource is to go for help to a mother with children. Most mothers would be willing to help another child find help. This is a good time to remind your walker about safe houses and neighborhood safe spots. Stress that the child should never go to a parking lot, deserted area, or even into a bathroom when running from a stranger. It is too easy for the victimizer to follow unobserved to those areas. It is important that

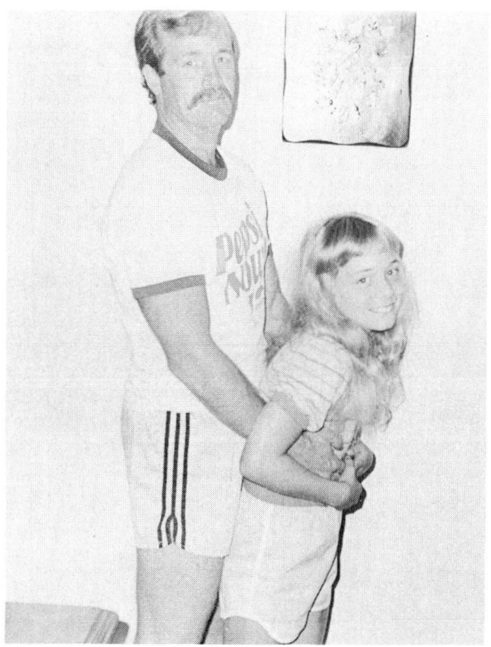

Always use an adult the child trusts as the victimizer when practicing self-defense, for example, the father, mother, or a teacher. It is much less frightening for the child.

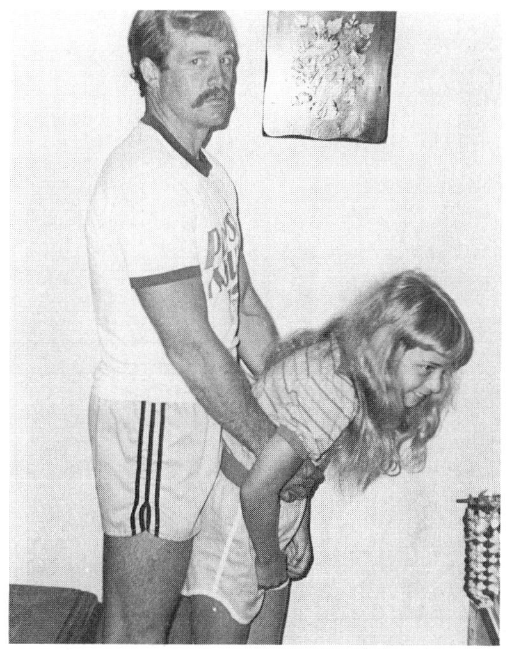

If a child is grabbed from behind, one defense move is instantly to slump forward relaxed.

you stress that it is better for the child to try to get quick help than to try to get home if threatened. The help can call and get the parent. The child who panics and tries to get home may be followed and will be more vulnerable to attack.

These physical techniques are last resorts. The best defense is still a good offense. Teach children to notice where they are walking, paying attention to the people around them, being aware of dangers ahead of time, knowing what to do if an initial contact is made, knowing their rights and what to do if they are violated; these practices are the first line of defense against victimizers.

Stranger Danger

Chapter 5 addresses the topic of strangers. The children should remember that strangers can look like anyone and that they do not go to nor talk to strangers without parental or caregiving adult's permission. A stranger who violates their rights is wrong. The situation needs to be changed by their saying NO, telling

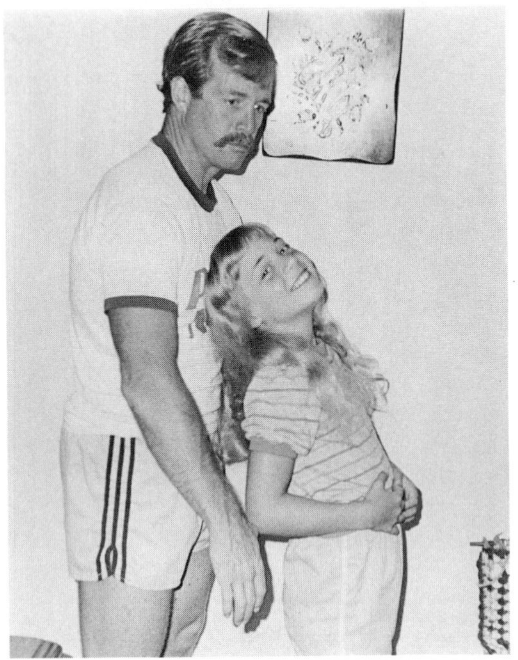

Then the child sharply swings his or her head into the solar plexis (midchest) of the grabber.

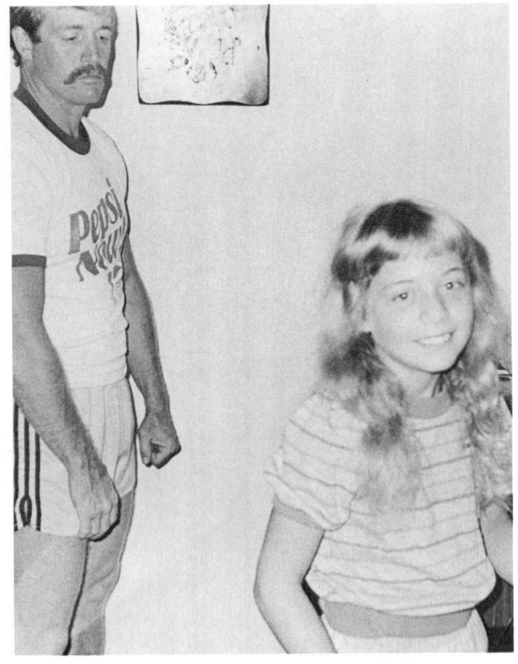

The child should run and yell the special yell at the very instant the grabber drops his or her hands.

a trusted adult, getting a buddy to stick up with them or, by other techniques. Now is the time to talk about strangers who are people we know or perceive we know; or, how to deal with strangers who are too friendly and friends who are not friends.

Now is the time to also build on the children's knowledge of stranger danger at the door and on the telephone. Remind children that strangers can be tricky but that they can be superduper detectives and keep a tricky stranger from catching them by using their smarts. Teach children a few basic sentences to use if someone comes to the door or telephones and an adult is not home or readily available. A few suggested sentences might be the following.

Examples

"I'll check on that; please wait out here."

"My mommy is busy now; she'll call you back later."

"Dad is in the shower; please call back later."

"Please leave the package; mom is too busy to come to the door now."

"Please call back later" with no explanation needed.

Children should be taught *never* to open the door without adult permission; this is the first line of home defense. Give children permission not to go to the door if they feel fearful. With the child, practice the types of reasons a victimizer might try to use to coerce or frighten the child to open the door; after each reason, reinforce that the door stays shut or the telephone gets hung up with no information relayed, especially if the child is home alone. Some common ploys of which your detective should be aware include the following:

Examples

"Mommy sent me to get you."

"You remember me; I'm Dad's friend."

"Mommy is hurt. I've come to take you to her. Hurry!"

"I'm hurt. Can I use the phone?"

"My dog is lost or stuck in your garage." Pets are often used as an excuse.

Practice these and any other ploys you can think of. Talk about each ploy and what would be an appropriate response. Do not forget to mention phoney uniforms that some abusers wear to try to confuse children. If a uniformed person comes to the door, the child should never open the door. Adults should check credentials *before* opening the door. Call the company or precinct to check on the person's authenticity. If it is a legitimate errand, the person will not mind. Do not call a telephone number the person gives because it could be a phoney telephone number. You do not need to tell a young child all of this, but adults should use caution. The child should refer to an adult and not open the door. If the parent is not home, the child can call a telephone friend or neighbor who can quickly come to the door and handle the adult at the door if the child is fearful or unsure of what to do.

Also review how people could know the names of the family. Mailboxes, mail, and the telephone book are possible sources. Remember that people who victimize children usually set up the situation and the child. It is rarely a one-shot attempt done on the spur of the moment. When interviewed, jailed child molesters said that they usually checked out children, tried to get their trust as a friend, and then made sexual advances slowly and subtly. Some molesters admitted using uniforms as a quick ploy to gain a child's confidence. They also studied the family and tried to fit with the child as if they were an old family friend. Molesters often cased the child and had information that could make an unsuspecting child believe that the molester is a family friend or safe person. The child should be aware of these ploys and know what to do in given situations. Remember—the molester is relying on ignorance and innocence to get an objective—a child.

The interviewed molesters also talked about ease of entry into a house. Deadbolt locks, peepholes in doors, and window locks act as deterents to the more aggressive type of molester. One word of caution: never unlock the deadbolt door lock and rely on a storm door if a stranger knocks. In one instance, a nice-looking man came to the storm door and rang the bell where a young girl was babysitting. He said he was looking for his dog that was in the people's garage. The babysitter unlocked the bolt and opened the door to speak to him, secure in the knowledge that the storm door was locked. The man then sprang through the door that he had previously broken and attacked her in the kitchen. The screams of the frightened children and a neighbor coming in response kept this girl from being harmed.

Although most of this chapter discusses sexual victimization prevention, it is important for children to be aware that other types of victimization also need to be addressed—kidnapping and drug abuse.

Kidnapping

Kidnapping is most often done by a person the child knows. Unfortunately, kidnapping is often the result of a custodial battle, when one parent tries to punish the estranged or divorced spouse through the children. However, the children suffer the most. Kidnapped children often have to endure being friendless and living with new names, almost as fugitives, as well as with the false belief that the other parent is dead or did not want them. This type of existence is psychologically damaging for the child. The other type of kidnapping is apt to be a professional kidnapper or a stranger who has become friendly with your child. These types of kidnappings often occur at malls, in movie houses, or in parks or school yards after hours.

It is difficult to prevent a kidnapping, but discussion and forewarning children may be the best preventions—along with common sense.

For good common sense, the parent or caregiver should reinforce safety skills with the children and be cautious in public places. Never leave children unattended in a car or a mall. Do not trust a stranger who looks nice to watch your children while you run into a store. Know who has your children and where they are bringing them. Know the route your children take home from school and how long it takes to get home. Reinforce all the safety skills that we have gone over and tell your children that no matter what anyone might tell them, you always want them and love them. Make sure the children learn to make a long distance and a collect call so they could call you from anywhere. Talk about where children could go if someone did take them away.

Taking out a social security card and a passport for a child is another good move in safeguarding against kidnapping. To get a social security card, one is required to show a certified birth certificate and proof of the child's identity, for example, a school report card, library card, or medical bill with the child's name. Only one number is issued to a person and that number is issued for life. It would be involved and difficult for someone to fake all these safeguards.

To obtain a passport for a child, a parent or guardian must show his or her driver's license, a certified birth certificate for the child, two passport photographs, and a social security card or other positive identification for the child. If the child is thirteen or older, the child must come into the post office with the parent or guardian to get a passport. A passport is valid for five years. Since a person cannot leave the country legally without a passport, it would be difficult to take a child out of the country if a passport has been applied for by the parents prior to a kidnapping situation. This safeguard is not foolproof, but does add an edge of safety.

Other precautions are to keep fingerprints, face-front pictures, identifying information, and descriptions of your children on hand at home. This information can be given to the police immediately if you suspect a kidnapping. The first twenty-four to forty-eight hours are said to be crucial. The more quickly information can be given to the police, the more likely that a recovery can be made. Several organizations now help people in this horrible situation. Hopefully, training and prior discussion can help prevent some kidnappings.

Drug Abuse

Drug abuse is another area in which a bigger child or an adult tries to victimize children. Taking milk money in exchange for "happy" pills is not just a high school or college problem. Child pushers are trying to get children into drugs at younger and younger ages. These pushers use threats and ignorance to get young children involved.

Talking frankly about taking pills, medicine, alcohol, and their related dangers with young children is a natural extension of learning about good health. If we are teaching children to beware of sugar and other items, then adding information about drugs is easy. Most of what they learn about victimizers is that they are bullies. If someone is giving the child a red light feeling, then the child needs to yell NO and tell. Telling on a drug pusher falls into the same category. This person is trying to make children do something bad, and they have the right to get help. It is important to reinforce that drugs are not a grown-up habit but are wrong and bad for people. A pusher often says that taking pills or smoking pot will make children be like grown-ups. This argument does appeal to children.

One word of caution: Do not preach about drugs. Tell the truth and let the children know that they have to make choices; the best choice is to say NO and tell. Scare tactics and preaching have not seemed to be nearly as effective a deterent as giving the facts and placing responsibility on the child as to ways to handle the drug problem. You may want to teach the child some sentences to use to say NO. Some sentences might be the following responses:

Examples
"Thanks, but no thanks."

"I'm not interested."

"I'm not into that stuff."

"Get lost."

Anything that helps the child say NO is helpful. Reinforcing the poison learnings also helps teach the drug problem. Drugs are poisons to your system unless taken as a prescription under a doctor's care. Level with children; say that drugs may feel good at first but that later the drugs cause a lot of damage. If you tell children that taking drugs doesn't feel good and they do try it and find it feels good, your credibility is gone. Keeping an eye on who your children's friends are and what they are into is also a good drug deterent.

Be aware that many items around the house are drugs; keep these away from children as you would any poison. Never refer to medications as candy or by cute names. Treat medications seriously and children will follow your example.

There has been an increase in children's use of typewriter fluid as an inhalant. Keep that item away from children as you would airplane glue and other substances that cause highs and can and have caused serious health problems. Let children know that use of these substances in an abusive manner is dangerous. Giving factual information is the best way to help children help themselves.

If you suspect a child may being using drugs or inhalants, call and get help. Do not wait until the problem becomes overwhelming. Denial is a normal initial reaction whenever people face unpleasant possibilities, but the only real solution is to face problems squarely and with good support and back-up. You can talk to the pediatrician, clergy, hotline people, and others. The most important thing is to act sensibly and quickly for the sake of the child.

ADULT RESPONSIBILITIES

The responsibility of a teacher, community worker, social worker and/or other people working with young children to report suspected sexual, physical, or emotional abuse varies greatly from state to state. If you are a professional, check your state's laws in this regard. If you are a parent, you should know what the laws demand of the professionals who deal with your child.

In Massachusetts there is a chapter 119, section 51A of the general laws that mandates professionals in the teaching, medical, firefighting, police, and social service fields to report suspected abuse cases to the state for investigation. The state Department of Social Services provides a packet of information so mandated reporters are aware of what to report, how to report, and what the follow-up procedures will be. There is a fine for noncompliance.

A call to the local Department of Social Services or Mental Health Association should direct you to the information you need. If your state has no laws protecting children by some type of reporting and investigative system, check into why and support the groups trying to establish them. The last chapter discusses why these laws are so important.

No matter what the laws are, teachers and other professionals need to be supportive and caring to children who have been or are being abused or neglected. The parents will also often seek out and need support. Do you know where in your city or town to direct them for professional help? Check your *Yellow Pages* and your agencies. Keep their telephone numbers handy. Also have on hand names of the few good books on the subject to which you can refer the parents. The teacher often is a first link in the reporting chain. This is true because the children often display the reactive behavior in the safety of the classroom or feel safe enough to come to a sensitive teacher and tell. It is important that you do not push the children away or avoid the subject. Often the initial disclosure is the tip of the iceberg. The children test you first to see if you can handle the problem and assure themselves that you will not think they are "bad." How you handle the children's first attempt to communicate is *vital.* Listen with undivided attention. Never try to speak for the children or put interpretations on what they are saying. You need to reassure them that what happened was not their fault. They are not bad. They did the right thing coming to you, and you will help.

If on your own without the child's disclosure (or even with the child's denial) you believe an abuse is evident, then you need to start documenting your suspicions with dates and notation. These notes will be invaluable later during an investigation, if one becomes warranted. For example, if a child has many falls with injury or bruises in odd places, the injuries should be documented. Perhaps the child is going through an awkward stage or has had a series of crazy accidents; such accidents may also signify abuse, especially if the accidents continue. Most often, you will be asked for some written back-up for your suspicions, which can be part of the daily write-ups most teachers do on their classes.

A well-written law does exempt the teacher or mandated reporter from liability if a suspected abuse report was made in good faith regardless of the investigative outcome. Sometimes a program has a procedure for reporting suspected abuse in which the worker or teacher is to report to a supervisor, principal, or director who, in turn, files the legal complaint. Sometimes, the school nurse or physician carries the ball with preliminary checks with the home and parents. You should know what is expected of you in your position.

INDICATORS OF NEGLECT AND ABUSE

Indicators of Child Neglect

1. Lack of supervision: young children left alone or under the care of other children who are too young.
2. Lack of appropriate clothing or hygiene: children who regularly are dirty and unwashed, have skin problems due to this situation, and/or are not dressed appropriately for the weather.
3. Lack of medical, dental, and nutritional care: decaying teeth, poor health, and insufficient food quality or quantity.
4. Lack of shelter: children housed in dangerous or unsanitary home conditions, such as having no heat.

Indicators of Physical Abuse

1. Bruises and welts: facial; on infants, many bruises in various stages or unusual patterns.
2. Burns: rope burns on hands, arms, or legs; cigarette burns; circle burns or immersion burns on limbs or gluteus maximus or genitals.
3. Cuts: eyes, any part of infant; any to genitals.
4. Skeleton or bone injury: internal injuries; apt more to be picked up by medical personnel.
5. Head or hair injuries: bald spots or red spots from pulled hair; jerky eye movements from abuse to head; missing or loose teeth at inappropriate ages.

Indicators of Sexual Abuse

1. Behavioral: unwilling to dress or undress with other children, withdrawn behavior or sexually sophisticated above age level, poor social skills.
2. Physical: trouble walking, sitting, and with lower body movement; torn or stained undergarments; bruised or bleeding from genitals and/or anus; pain or itching when urinating or defecating; venereal disease.

CHILD SEXUAL ABUSE FACT SHEET

Who?

Usually young children between the ages of two and six are initially approached by molesters who take advantage of their innocence.

By Whom?

By adults who use the child as a focal point for their own problems. Ninety percent are men with no certain pattern or stereotype. About eighty percent are *known* to the child; abusers are *not strangers.*

How Prevalent?

It is estimated that one in four girls will be molested before age eighteen and one in six boys will also be molested before age eighteen. These are conservative estimates.[15]

What Is Meant by Sexual Abuse?

Sexual abuse is a sexual act imposed through trickery or force on a child under age eighteen who lacks the emotional, cognitive, and/or maturational development necessary for consent.

Kinds of Sexual Abuse

Rape: a violent act initiated by an assailant who forces the victim to perform sexual acts by a threat or use of force and without consent of the victim.
Blitz rape: a sudden rape without warning.
Confidence rape: a rape when the victimizer uses trickery or gains access to the victim by betrayal. Often uses violence.

Incest: any form of sexual activity between a child and parent, stepparent, extended family member, or surrogate parent.

Sexual misuse: any sexual stimulation inappropriate for the child's age; may not be abusive as by the definition given above.

15. Central Mass. Camp Fire et al., 2.

What Is the Common Pattern of Confidence Rape or Abuse?

It is most common for an initial contact or suggestion to be made before an actual attack or abuse situation.

Who Is Most Likely to be a Victim? Who Is Least Likely?

Children who react quietly and fearfully to an initial contact are most likely to be victimized. Their inability to handle a subtle or overt suggestion due to lack of knowledge or preparation makes these children more susceptible. A child who says NO and tells is most likely to avoid being a victim. Most abusers do *not* want people to know that they are up to something. They are looking for the lone or easily intimidated child. Often, victims of child sexual abuse are abused for a period of years until adolescence before they realize that the situation is wrong or not their fault and/or before they tell someone. Early training can make a tremendous difference.

Signs of Possible Sexual Abuse Physical

Veneral disease: A certain indicator
Pregnancy: A certain indicator
Foreign bodies in rectum or vagina
Bruises in genital, rectal areas, or chest or abdomen
Bleeding from genital or rectal areas
Problems with urinary system

Emotional

Fear of certain places, people, or night disturbances
Depression, withdrawal
Poor peer relationships
"Sexy" behavior above age level; inappropriate acting out
Running away

What to Do if a Child Comes to You Saying He or She Is Being Abused

1. Listen to the child. Do not lead the child.
2. Bring the child to a physician for a physical examination if you are the parent.
3. Talk to the family if you are the teacher and report suspected abuse to proper authorities.

Stay *calm!* Do *not frighten* the child! Support the child's feelings! Contact local rape crisis center or counseling center! *Help is available;* you are not on your own! Report to the authorities; victimizers will and do continue to abuse other children, too!

SIGNS OF POSSIBLE DRUG ABUSE IN YOUNG CHILDREN

The symptoms can mimic a flu or even a cold or allergy. If a child is acting lethargic with no medical symptoms forthcoming, the cause could be drug related. If a child is withdrawing, suddenly changing a group of friends, or overreacting severely to normal stress, there is a chance the child is involved with drugs. You need to exercise caution because many other medical and developmental situations can cause the same reactions. You are really looking for a pattern of sudden behavioral or physical changes. School grades can also be an indicator of a new stress in the child's life. Sudden swings or slumps in grades usually have a reason. Sudden mood swings also are a good indicator of a social or a drug problem. Being open and aware can make a big difference in helping the child with a drug problem. Try to keep up on what is important to your child, what is causing problems, and be a good listener. Other possible signs include:

1. Stuttered or stammered speech
2. Red eyes or blurry eyes
3. Spacey look with a seeming lack of focus
4. Excessive defensiveness
5. Missing articles, money, or medications
6. Sudden lack of appetite

Remember: You are not alone. You can call any drug-related hot line for information or help. Many fine books on this subject can inform and direct you in the right way to proceed. Local parent support groups can also be of great help.

CHILDREN'S RIGHTS ABOUT VICTIMIZATION PREVENTION

1. You have the right to trust your feelings.
2. You have the right to say NO loudly and clearly whenever you have the red light feeling.
3. You have the right to say NO to a bigger child or an adult.
4. You have the right to tell if anyone, even a friend, makes you feel the red light feeling.
5. You have the right *not* to keep bad secrets.
6. You have the right to be believed.
7. You have the right to keep telling until you are believed. Tell mom, dad, teacher, clergy, school nurse, doctor until you are believed.
8. You have the right to defend yourself the best way you can when you feel threatened, scared, or have the red light feeling. This includes doing nothing.
9. You have the right to decide who can come into your personal space and when.
10. You have the right to your privacy when you want or need it.
11. You have the right to be respected for your wishes.
12. Other people also have the right to their personal space and privacy. You should respect their rights, too!
13. You have the right to be loved for yourself and cared for by your caregiving adults.
14. You have the right to think *before* doing anything about which you feel unsure.

Remember: A right is not a privilege. Children have a right to be fed but not to demand pizza. That is a privilege. Rights deal with basic things in life and do not mean that children can ask for or get whatever they want.

KEY WORDS FOR PARENTS

Red light feeling: Sit down, let supper burn, and listen, really listen. Your child is mixed up or has a problem that needs to be shared with you.

Green light feeling: Good feelings about or toward someone or something.

Good touch: Touches that feel good to the child, that are welcomed and that are proper touches for young children.

Confusing touch: Touches that start out feeling all right or even good but then change and are no longer welcomed or feel good or safe.

Bad touch: Touches that are hurtful or make the child feel sad or upset.

Telling: When a child tells to help himself or herself or a friend.

Tattling: When a child tells to get someone in trouble; does not help anyone.
Telephone friend: Someone you trust who lives nearby and who your child can call in an emergency or if frightened.
Special yell: A deep-from-the-toes yell that children are taught to use in an emergency or if they feel threatened.
Good secret: A secret that eventually gets shared and makes people happy—such as a birthday surprise.
Bad secret: A secret that is not supposed to get told *ever* and makes the child feel bad, upset, or angry. This secret needs to be told to a safe adult right away.
Safe adult: Usually the parents; also includes teachers, clergy, and/or other trusted adults. Children need to know they can go to an alternate adult in case one of the safe people is the perpetrator or cause of the problem.

UNCLE HARRY AND AMY[16]

Amy is a little girl your age. One Saturday morning, Amy's parents had to go out of town. They took her over to her aunt and uncle's house to spend the day. After her parent's drove away, Amy went into the living room and did what lots of kids do on Saturday mornings. What would that be?

Yes, she turned on the television to watch cartoons. While she was sitting there Aunt Mary came in to tell her she was going to the store and would be back in a little while. Aunt Mary said to Amy, "Now if you need anything, just call your uncle. He's upstairs working. I'll be back in an hour."

Amy was sitting there having a good time watching TV when Uncle Harry came downstairs. He came over and sat next to her and asked her what she was watching. "Just cartoons," Amy said. Uncle Harry leaned over and turned off the TV. He said he hadn't seen her in a long time and she could watch cartoons any Saturday. Then, Uncle Harry said, "Why don't you come and sit closer to me?" He patted his thigh. Amy moved her chair closer about two inches. But Uncle Harry wanted her to sit even closer so he said (sternly), "Over here young lady!" Amy started to feel very uncomfortable. She squirmed in her chair and looked away.

"Now that's better" said Uncle Harry, "you're getting to be such a big girl, Amy, how old are you? You're getting to be so pretty." And Uncle Harry started rubbing her back and petting her hair. In a very small voice, Amy said, "I'm eight years old." She looked down to the ground. Then Uncle Harry took her hand and put it on his leg. He moved it back and forth. Now Amy was real scared. She didn't like how he was touching her. And she didn't want to touch his leg.

16. Camp Fire Girls et al., *Children's Awareness Training.*

Uncle Harry was still talking, "I'll bet you're a help to your Mom around the house." Amy nodded slowly, squirming in her chair.

"Did you see that movie, ET, Amy?" "Yes!" said Amy. "Well," said Uncle Harry, "I'll bet you'd like an ET T-shirt." Amy thought about the T-shirt and smiled a small smile as she thought of the shirt. "Yes," she said. "I'll tell you what, Amy," Uncle Harry said as he leaned forward, "If you give your favorite uncle a great big kiss, he'll be sure to get you a T-shirt." Now Amy wanted the T-shirt, but she didn't know about kissing Uncle Harry. "I said, a kiss, young lady!" Amy leaned over and gave her uncle a little kiss on the cheek, making a face the whole time. She looked away as fast as she could. He sure is acting weird, she thought.

"You liked that didn't you?" Uncle Harry asked. Amy didn't say anything out loud but inside she thought "Yuck." At that moment, Aunt Mary's car pulled into the driveway. Amy turned quickly to get up but Uncle Harry was faster and grabbed Amy by the arm. Pulling her face close to his, he said, "Now listen, Amy. I don't want anyone to know about this. This is our little secret. Do you understand?" Amy was scared and nodded a small nod.

Points for Discussion:

- How did the niece feel?
- Establish that she did not like or want to be touched in the way she was touched.
- Discuss the secret. Be sure the children understand what the secret was.
- Explore whom she could tell. Acknowledge that she might not be believed the first time but she should try again.
- Brainstorm ways that Amy could have handled the situation. Focus on getting away, saying NO, and telling.
- Acknowledge the difficulty in saying NO. What should she do? Rewrite the story as a success.

QUESTIONS FOR REVIEW

1. Who victimizes young children?
2. What are some common myths about young children?
3. What are the two strategies that lay the groundwork for training young children?
4. How do you build on the five senses to develop safety concepts with young children?
5. Explain the term *personal space.*
6. Name three role plays about bullies and young children.
7. Define tattling. Define telling.
8. How do you explain a bad secret to a child?
9. What kind of force can an adult use on a young child and why does it so often work?
10. What questions can children ask about a person's touching them?
11. What are the three kinds of touch we teach young children?
12. What are the correct names for the body parts that are private parts?
13. How can the red light, green light method help you test young children's understanding of the sexual victimization prevention learnings?
14. Name two self-defense moves that the young child can possibly learn and use.
15. To whom can a child turn for help?
16. Is kidnapping an abuse of a child? How?
17. Discuss two ways to help prevent kidnapping.
18. What are some signs of drug abuse in young children?
19. How can you help a child handle peer pressure about drugs?
20. How can a teacher or worker help an abused child after the child has disclosed the nature and perpetrator of the abuse?
21. Is your response to a child very important? Why?
22. Give two indicators of each of the following: neglect, physical abuse, sexual abuse.
23. What is rape? sexual misuse? incest?
24. Name three children's rights about victimization.

CHAPTER 7

Parent, Teacher, and Community Relations

Because parents are the primary caregivers to their children and the people who exercise the most influence over them during their younger years, the success of any program depends on parents who are actively involved. Teachers and community workers, especially those involved in all-day day-care situations, are also important. The two groups working together on mutually agreed training materials to help teach safety to young children results in the strongest influence to promote and reinforce the skills needed for safety training, insuring a higher success factor.

Today's parents are often bombarded with a lot of advice on how they should and should not parent. Magazines, books, and newspapers tell them how to raise a brighter child, for example, or how to get a head start on their child's future. As discussed in previous chapters, many of the traditional family supports are now missing. When added to the media blitz of contradictory parenting information, plus the economic realities of single-parent and working-parent families, this lack of support can add stress to parents' lives. Sometimes this stress results in parents who try to be superparents and give their children everything without considering themselves. Sometimes it results in parents who close their eyes and take care of themselves, often to the exclusion of their children's emotional needs. Sometimes it results in an inconsistent pattern of these two extremes.

Parents who are very busy can use help with safety training reinforcement. Older siblings can often fill this need. Just as younger children have learned many childhood rhymes and warnings from older children, they can practice

Role play and dramatization with young children may require adult help for set-up, but they should then move to child-to-child interactions. Parents and teachers act as facilitators, not directors.

safety role plays and situation options with them. Older children feel important and especially helpful with this responsibility. A word of warning: Make sure that the older child can handle this duty responsibly without getting overly enthusiastic or creative. Parents usually are good judges of their children and should choose carefully which sibling will be allowed to help with safety training. It is also a good idea to make frequent checks of how the training is going. Help from an older child does not eliminate the parent role. The parent is still the strongest support for the child being trained. This additional safety practice is a way of giving the child extra reinforcement even if the parent schedule is tight.

Older children are a valuable resource for safety training. Young children traditionally have learned from older children. This link is a terrific reinforcement for older children as well as a good learning experience for the younger ones.

Parents often say that they feel uncomfortable with sexual discussions with young children. To facilitate the discussions and keep both parent and child at ease, it is helpful to use dolls, teddy bears, or puppets as motivators. It is not necessary that the dolls be anatomically correct, but it is a good idea to keep in mind when buying dolls. It makes sense to have the doll exactly the same in structure as the child. Boys need and use dolls as well as girls. Role play as a father is a healthy and positive experience for young boys that is not always supported by parents as much as it should be. Play therapists often use dolls to facilitate child disclosures and discussions. Additional supports for discussions can be pictures from the family medical book, anatomy book pictures, and picture books for young children about their bodies. It is neither necessary nor advisable to actually show the child the adult body. Seeing the

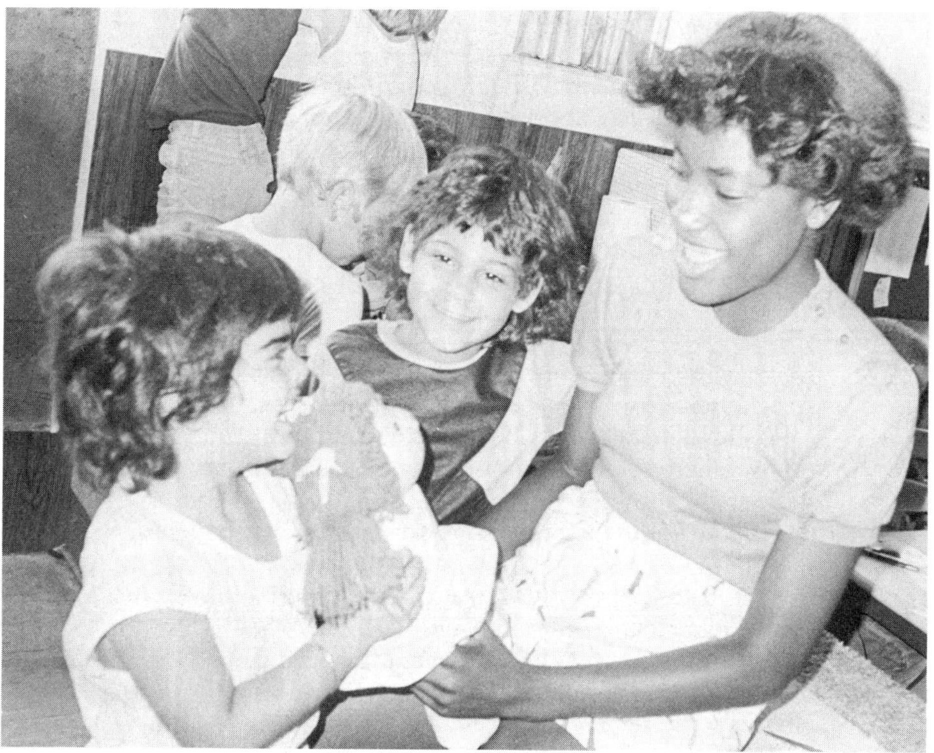

Dolls, teddy bears, and puppets are excellent conversation facilitators. They help adults feel more comfortable initiating conversations about safety. They obviously grab the children's interest.

adult by accident is a normal occurrence, but to force the issue is not in the child's best interest.

The teacher along with a pediatrician or nurse is often in the role of being a parent's liaison between accurate information about child rearing and help for a child's problem or recognition that there is, in fact, no real problem—just a normal child going through normal development stages. It is important that the teacher keep up on what is going on in the home and maintain good parent relations so the parents feel comfortable coming to the teacher for occasional help or direction. You may have a background in child development, but most other people do not. Few people take even one course in normal child development; there are people with doctorates in the position of being uneducated in child development. Parenting is one of the few responsibilities that require no formal or informal preparation. One can parent from age twelve or thirteen on. People often expect that the birth of their child will suddenly give them parental wisdom or motherly instincts. When this does not happen, many people feel frustrated; parenting is difficult, and that difficulty is often impossible to acknowledge, even to friends. How many people admit to a friend that they are having a problem with their child? In this age of smaller families and nuclear family structure, many parents have not seen or observed care of younger children at home, even during their own growing up years. Parents have no role models to whom they can turn.

COMMUNICATION

A teacher cannot and should not try to do everything. A good and sensitive teacher can, however, be a valuable resource. As a teacher, you know where to get brochures, you read teacher and child care magazines and books, and you know where community resources are available. Sharing this information with parents in a matter-of-fact manner and being a good listener for the parent in stress can strengthen the home-school bond and make life easier for parent and child.

Some teachers find it useful to maintain a folder with fact sheets on subjects of concern to parents. With each fact sheet, have the telephone number of a resource that parents can contact, titles of books parents can read, and titles of books they can read to children. This information can be easily copied and shared with all parents as an addition to your regular newsletter, or given out individually as needed or requested by a parent. Taking a few minutes before or after class to talk with a parent can open a nice relationship.

All too often, teachers and parents have rarely been communicating. This can be rectified by viewing your position of teacher or community worker as one of partnership with the parents; the parents can view their role in the same light. After all, we all have the same objective—the well-being of the children.

Communication can be opened in many ways. The teacher can send home newsletters that tell of the daily activities in the classroom, special events, and even recipes or ideas easily tried at home. Teachers can send home free, informative brochures received from local associations (e.g., auto safety groups, dental and medical associations). Schools or community groups can sponsor speakers and hold meetings about child rearing and discipline at convenient times for parents. Teachers can maintain a memo board on which they post information about child-rearing issues, cartoons about parenting and children, and updates on safety recalls for toys or children's equipment, for example. School-sponsored social get-togethers can also help involve some parents. Working parents often find it difficult to get to know the parents of their children's friends. Such social occasions offer this opportunity.

Parents can help in this partnership by offering suggestions, sharing materials to help support the program, offering verbal supports to the teachers, perhaps coming in and helping with the program in an area in which they have a particular expertise (e.g., making potato pancakes, working in clay, or showing the children about a job), or helping with trips or even performing day-to-day chores for which the teacher needs parental help.

The better the parent-teacher (community worker) relationship, the more in tune the harmony between school and home. The more open the shared communication, the less likely it is that problems will arise with the children in home or at school. With a firm and trusted foundation of understanding, the programs that are introduced, such as this safety program, are more likely to succeed and benefit the children.

A lack of understanding, trust, or communication can lead to resistance to trying new ideas and establishing the need for new directions in learning. Partnership attitudes can break down barriers and open the door for more enriched program development within the classrooms of young children.

CHILDREN'S RIGHTS: AN IMPORTANT ISSUE

Another way for parent, teachers, and community workers to come together is to recognize an issue's importance, and mutually work for change or promotion of the issue into the public arena. Nothing is stronger than a lobby of parents, teachers, and community workers when all are working toward a mutual goal.

Many important issues are coming to the fore in the area of early childhood education. Society is recognizing young children as a legitimate group of people entitled to the full protection under the Constitution's Bill of Rights. This represents a change from the perception of them as a subsection under parents to a fuller recognition of their own personhood. Until recently, abuses to children have left many people appalled, but the perpetrators are free because of constitutional or legal discrepancies and a lack of interpretation or precedent in how the victimizer should be handled. In the recent past, the only way a town could help an abused child was to call in the Society for the Prevention of Cruelty to Animals. Animal rights took precedence over children's rights. This new area of child rights will take sustained efforts on the part of all people concerned to continue the movement.

Children's rights and needs should be promoted in the public eye, the court rooms, and the halls of legislation. Adults concerned with the welfare of young children must act on influences that will change for the better the conditions of life for our children. Action-oriented avenues open to all adults include lobbying, writing to our elected and other political figures, working within support groups that promote children's rights and safety, and promoting with time, verbal support, and monies endeavors that help young children. The more people who become aware and informed about children's needs, the better the opportunity to move together to change our laws, strengthen their enforcement, and change perceptions about young children to a more realistic and safer vision.

In the United States, each state has its own laws that govern children and their rights. In general, these laws are archaic and relate to an era when children were considered to be of less value than a horse or a cart. In our society, which we consider civilized, it is appalling that some states regard child abuse as a misdemeanor even when it results in maiming or other severe injury. The larger view of the world shows clearly that people concerned with children's rights have an uphill fight. Not only is abuse increasing in the United States, but throughout the world as well. Demand for production of goods, for example, is causing a return to an old form of abuse in nations that have no child labor laws.

Many newspaper and television stories highlight "the seriousness of child abuse and neglect in the United States. Most people have no idea that it is one of the leading causes of death for children . . . . The International Labor Organization reports that the use of child labor throughout the world is increasing. More than fifty-five million children under fifteen years of age are being used as workers. Most of them are underpaid. Many work long hours in jobs that are hazardous or harmful to their health."[1] This illustrates the importance of reaffirming our committment to protect our children from falling through the cracks as society changes. This alarming pattern of abuse in our society should stir people to the fight for children's rights.

TACKLING THE PROBLEM

A three-pronged attack is necessary to change the current status of young children's rights. The first part is a comprehensive safety program for children and their parents; education in parenting skills would also strengthen this area. The second part consists of strengthening the existing licensing laws and codes and instituting a system of supervising these laws that is more vigilant and uniform throughout the nation. The third area of attack is an active public campaign of awareness to pressure our legal system to adopt new and fairer definitions and interpretations of children and their rights. We need to erase the old laws that consider children as chattel.

1. Margaret O. Hyde, *Cry Softly, the Story of Child Abuse* (Philadelphia: Westminster Press, 1980), 67.

Safety Education

The first area of attack has begun. Television, books, speakers, and educators are speaking out about the need for parenting education. Camp Fire Girls, scouting organizations, and community service programs are all organizing and executing basic awareness skill programs for children and their families. Police departments are running special safety programs for school-aged children. We need more public and private support for continuing existing safety programs and for creating new programs. We need to lower the age of the children protected by such programs of safety training to include children from two years old and up. Many programs begin in elementary school; however, children are often most at risk prior to school age.

USA Cable Network twice daily features a show called "Alive and Well," which focuses on children's issues and safety. These shows are based on a feature of the same name in *Family Circle Magazine.* Many young parents read this inexpensive magazine, which is available in supermarkets. The March 6, 1984, issue featured an article entitled, "Teach Your Kids to Protect Themselves." This article explained how parents could act out handling many situations with their children. This type of positive and informative advice is valuable to use with children and provides an opportunity to practice skills learned in the curriculum.

Dr. T. Berry Brazelton has written many good books about child rearing and parenting education. He has trained many of the country's finest young pediatricians, and Dr. Benjamin Spock has endorsed his approaches to child care. "Now Brazelton has brought his expertise and easy going charm to television. He's the host of Lifetime's *What Every Baby Knows,* an innovative half-hour series that focuses on child development from birth to age three. The show addresses such common problems as crying, toilet training and tantrums, as well as more complicated issues of single parenting, premature infants and overly active children.

'The show is not only very instructive, but it is also supportive for parents who are dealing with these issues,' says Brazelton."[2] This type of programming is vital. Young parents are rarely trained for parenting, the most important job of their lives. Few parents or grandparents are around to offer support in our restructuring society. "'It's a stressed lifestyle and parents need to have good backup for their children. And these days I don't know if they can always find it.'"[3]

The Children's Museum in Boston is another positive parent and child support in our society. The museum offers hands-on fun and learning for young children. The children are encouraged to touch everything. The museum also boasts a wonderful infant and toddler environment. According to Amy Squibb,

2. Rex Morgan, "Focus On: Dr. T. Berry Brazelton," *The Cable Guide* (June 1984), 28–29.
3. Morgan, 28–29.

an early childhood educator and consultant at the Boston Children's Museum, the environment with its adjoining parent learning room has become a focal point for young and older parents to meet, share child-raising problems, and learn together. Parents need to find this kind of support system regardless of their socioeconomic background. Ms. Squibb commented on how interesting it is to see people from all backgrounds and life-styles enjoying their children together at the museum, sharing stories and coffee. This center can lead the way for more such centers to be developed.[4]

Some libraries are beginning to shift focus of their story hours; parents are staying to talk. These meetings would make a good starting point in many communities for a parent support group.

Licensing Child-Care Facilities

Much needs to be done in the area of licensing for day-care and child-care centers. Many new day-care centers are opening to meet the needs of today's parents. But not all day-care centers are good. Some are not legal and do not meet minimum safety standards. Not all of the people staffing these centers are competent. Unfortunately, such situations have already had tragic consequences because society's need has outstripped its legal and moral adjustment. Society now needs to address a new set of requirements to provide safe and healthy environments for our young children.

The National Association for the Education of Young Children, an organization of concerned early childhood educators and parents, has addressed these issues and needs for the past few years. The organization is trying to promote a code of ethics and standards for people working with young children and to lobby for changes within the legal system to support young children. The organization also promotes the annual Week of the Young Child to increase public and corporate awareness of children's issues. Your support of their endeavors and your input can be of great help.

One problem has been a lack of trained personnel to supervise the current and new programs. The Councils for Children and other agencies have been actively pushing for an increase in the number of both child advocates and licensing agents within the Office for Children structure. If your state does not have an Office for Children, call your state representative and find out which agency has jurisdiction for children's rights and well-being. Contact that agency and work with it on updating laws and regulations.

The local Council for Children is open to care providers, parents, and any interested adults. The Council tries to investigate children's needs, family needs,

4. Amy Squibb, "Growing Together Outside the Home," Citizen's Resource Center Workshop, University of Massachusetts Medical School, January 21, 1984.

and quality of programs; to keep up with new legislation; to lobby for positive bills; to publish relevant information; and to provide training opportunities. In short, this action-oriented council is facilitating positive change for children. Attend a meeting of your local council; get involved. If you cannot commit the time, then become aware of the programs and legislation being promoted and write letters in their support.

In general, education and safety standards need to become nationally uniform. A teacher should be expected to fill the same requirements throughout the nation. The hierarchy of teacher aide, teacher, head-teacher, director, and owner/operator should be standard, with well-defined job qualifications and job descriptions that are consistent. These standards are particularly important within the child day-care community.

We need to promote changes that will provide at least minimum competency standards for the people caring for our next generation, at least minimum safety and building standards for the buildings that will house these programs, at least some minimum level of curriculum development for the centers of care, and a uniform and active supervisory agency to enforce these standards. In these ways we can eliminate some of the problems that now plague the educational system that is now in operation. It is time for change.

Public Relations and Laws

The last area of attack is in the public relations and legal arena. There is a close correlation between what happens in congress and legislative bodies and the desires of the public and press. Lately, television programs have pointed up some of the more dramatic problems with the present legal system and our current problems with abuse, kidnapping, and molestation. Our laws do not always protect our children. In fact, some laws hinder the safety and well-being of young children.

The legal system in the United States is largely based on the British system that provides for an accused person to have the right of confrontation with the accuser and the right to trial by a jury. Our legal system provides the accused molester or abuser with the right of face-to-face confrontation with the accuser, cross-examination, and trial by jury in a courtroom. These concepts can and do cause justice to miscarry for many cases involving young children.

According to Rape Crisis figures, before the average sexual molester is brought to trial he or she has already victimized about sixty children. The average child abuse offender threatens the young child with some type of retribution. Imagine the three- or four-year-old child sitting in the courtroom across from the adult who not only victimized the child but also threatened retribution. Imagine the child calmly telling what happened, recalling minute details for the attorneys, judge, and jury, and handling the pressure of cross-examination.

Kee MacFarlane, a child abuse counselor in the McMartin School case (the McMartin School of Manhattan Beach, California, is currently embroiled in a case of child molesting its charges for pornographic reasons), said that her interviews with more than 250 current and former McMartin students revealed a 10-year reign of terror, complete with death threats against the children and their families and the killing of animals in front of the children. "They're so easily bribed and so easily tricked," said Ms. MacFarlane, adding that some children believe the jailed defendants "can bend the bars and get out of jail."[5] Because of this present legal situation, even when an accused abuser or molester is caught with a preponderance of evidence, "Prosecuter, parent and therapist agreed that it is sometimes better to let a molester go free than to force children to testify in court."[6] This testimony was part of much delivered to law makers in Washington, D.C., at a senate panel investigating the juvenile justice system. It emphasizes the horror of the child's present position within our legal system. The child becomes a double victim in the effort to prevent an abuser from abusing other children. Solutions must be found to eliminate this situation.

In Los Angeles, Deputy District Attorney Lael Rubin, together with Kee MacFarlane and other people, is trying to have the children's testimony in the McMartin School case put onto closed-circuit television that will be admissible in the court. Rubin and the others believe that the children "whose lives have already been shattered from having had to face the defendants" would be put in a situation in which "no purpose could be served by having them as witnesses."[7]

The use of modern technology can protect the child from having to face a victimizer. Its use allows for the exercise of a victim's right to confront the accuser but tempers that right with prudence. This law and others need to be examined and revised to become more just for the children. This case in California is by no means isolated. It does show that vague laws, lax regulations and enforcement, and ignorance of safety aids bred conditions that allowed this kind of victimization to persist for ten years.

THE NEED FOR SAFETY EDUCATION

As both a teacher and a parent, I have spoken with many parents. Mothers have said they hate to see television news broadcasts or read the newspapers, which seem every evening to highlight stories of child kidnapping, rape, and abuse. Parents find it difficult to think that their child sweetly dreaming in bed could

5. "Victim, 9, on Rapist: Jail Him," *The Evening Gazette* (Worcester, Mass.), (May 2, 1984).
6. "Victim . . . ."
7. "Victim . . . ."

be a victim of a crime or tragedy. It is all too easy to push away these horrible thoughts, shut off the television, and think that at least their child is safe.

This, however, is a false security—*no child is safe* when these conditions exist. Eventually, all children are away from direct parental control. You might trust the wrong person. You might turn away from your child for an instant in a shopping mall or in the park. The opportunity for a tragedy could present itself.

How many parents who are trying to restore a child's ego after an attack also felt that it could not happen to their child? How many parents waiting to hear from a lost or missing child felt that same way? This is the price for our false security and our children's ignorance for their own protection. Knowledge that is cope-oriented, age-appropriate, and competently administered does not "give ideas" nor does it "spoil our children's innocence." Knowledge can prevent tragedies by preparing the children for these situations. Knowledge brings strength and trust. Public awareness and discussions bring the problem into the open.

The time to safeguard our children is *now!* Use this curriculum as a starting point. Add to it; change it; use it over and over. Actively encourage and support existing programs that promote children's awareness training and safety skill development. Support local organizations that are trying to address these problems—police, fire, YWCA, YMCA, Girl Scouts, Boy Scouts, Camp Fire Girls, 4-H, and others. Be aware! Read the newspaper! Write and/or call your elected and appointed officials! Let them know your concerns! Join together with other people in groups such as the Local Council for Children where your concerns can force needed changes to protect our children. There is power in numbers, power enough to fight for the powerless and win!

One voice crying out may be heard; many voices together can shatter illusions, making us face and find real solutions for the problems around us. *Be one of those voices! Make a difference!*

TEN WAYS TO BRIDGE THE COMMUNICATION GAP BETWEEN PARENTS AND CHILDREN

1. Begin by learning to listen to yourself.
2. Be available.
3. Give of yourself rather than giving money.
4. Do things together with your children.
5. Be informed.
6. Give in on minor issues so you can hold out on major ones.
7. Be generous with honest praise.
8. Give mental as well as physical privacy.

9. Set a good example.
10. Be a parent, not a pal.

Sometimes we all get so busy that we neglect to make time, to slow down and be there just to talk. Mom runs to her job, her club, and her friends; the children follow busy schedules of school, dance, sports, and religious classes. Dad has his job and its commitments, his golf game, and trips. One mother said she realized how busy everyone was when her five-year-old asked on a Friday if she could talk to her on Monday afternoon. Later, later quickly becomes a way of life. Does your child need to make an appointment to see you?

TIME-OUT TIPS FOR PARENTS UNDER STRESS

All parents occasionally lose patience with their children. Some parents choose the wrong technique for handling the situation. Next time you feel you are losing patience, try one of these stress reducers *before handling the situation or your child:*

1. Walk out of the room and count to 100.
2. Put on your favorite album or tape and wait until it is over before doing anything.
3. Telephone a friend with a child about the same age and talk about the problem.
4. Write down all the good points of your child on a piece of paper.
5. Take a hot bath and mull over the problem.
6. Write down all the ways you could handle this situation.
7. Vacuum the house or polish the furniture.
8. Go out for a jog or a walk in the fresh air. Listen for the birds and sounds of nature. Go for a bike ride.
9. Send your child to his or her room and sit down with a cup of hot tea and a good book or magazine.
10. Play Bill Cosby's tape "Himself" and have a good laugh. Laughter helps put matters into perspective.
11. Stop and think! Does this problem really matter? Is it really earth shattering? Will the world come to an end over this incident?
12. Exercise.

Now you are ready to handle the situation calmly and with adult restraint. What a wonderful example you will be for your developing and learning child on how to handle anger and upsets. If you still need help, call your local parent stress Hot Line, take a course in child growth and development or child behavior, or get professional help. Do this especially if you often have difficulty handling your anger. Help is available.

Discipline Code BECKER JUNIOR COLLEGE Early Childhood Ed.

1. No child will be allowed to harm another child, an adult, or a classroom pet.
2. No child will be allowed to destroy property.
3. No hitting or any other physical force will be used on a child in this program.
4. No yelling will be used at children! A firm, quiet voice with a *low pitch* will be used when disciplining.
5. No threats or unenforceable warnings will be issued.
6. All children will be disciplined consistently with the minimum intervention of staff as a given situation demands. We are trying to foster self-discipline.
7. Accusatory statements and negatives will not be addressed to the child but to the undesirable behavior itself. Positive statements to the child will still be used.
8. Children will be taught and encouraged to verbalize anger rather than to use unacceptable physical aggressive reactions.
9. Intervention shall be the first step, if possible, with follow-up discussion.
10. Positive reinforcement protects the child's developing personality while still clarifying what is or is not acceptable behavior.
    eg.: "No, I cannot allow you to hit Jane. I realize that you are angry but people *are not for hitting.* You are special and I care about you. I will not let anyone hit you, but I also care about Jane so I can't allow you to hit her, either. Did you tell her that you are angry? Let's talk it over with her and see what we can come up with."
11. Sometimes it may be necessary to have a time-out period to cool off and allow the child to regain enough self-control to discuss the situation. Time-outs will be no longer than necessary to calm down. A child will be told that he or she can leave the time-out place as soon as he or she feels ready to listen or has regained control.
12. Recurring behavior may mean a temporary denial of a piece of equipment or activity; i.e., throwing sand at the sand box repeatedly could result in a child's not being allowed to play in the sandbox until the next time we come out to play. A substitute activity will be offered to facilitate transition.
13. In the very rare instance of repeated and wide-range unacceptable behavior, an individualized behavior modification plan will be implemented with parental approval.

Any questions in regard to specifics may be directed to either Mrs. Comer, Director, or Mrs. Brisebois, Teacher. The Director has time to help any parent with specific behavior problems that may develop. Please feel free to call on her.

Unacceptable Social Behaviors

Hitting	Swearing	Spitting	Destruction of property	Scratching
Biting	Throwing	Kicking	Body throwing (i.e., head butts, etc.)	Bullying

Our Social Studies Program will cover Good Mental Health and Emotional Development.
Emotions: recognition, validation of feeling, acceptable and unacceptable expressions of emotions.

In a discussion-type atmosphere, the following emotions will be explored: happy, sad, angry, frustrated, proud, frightened, and loved. We will discuss what makes the child feel that way, what he or she does to make others feel that way, and how I let others know how I feel.

Later in the year, we will be discussing personal rights and safety, including victimization prevention in positive, nonthreatening manners. In our curriculum, it is important that we wait to discuss victimization prevention until the children have been exposed to body parts and general and street safety, and until a level of basic trust and comfort has been established.

FIGURE 7.1
Sample discipline code.

WAYS THAT KIDS TELL SOMEONE THEY NEED HELP[8]

Often telling will not be in words, but by a change in behavior. Since children are not usually able to tell directly, it helps to be sensitive to their signals

- A child may be reluctant to go to a particular place or with a particular person.
- A child may show an unusual interest in the genitals of other people or of animals. S/he may try to express affection in inappropriate ways, such as "french kissing" or fondling of a parent's genitals.
- The child may be diagnosed as having a venereal disease . . . .
- Other signals can include:
  sleep disturbances (nightmares, bedwetting, fear of sleeping alone, needing a nightlight)
  loss of appetite or sudden increase in appetite
  lots of new fears—needing more reassurance than in the past
  returning to younger, more babyish behavior
  suddenly turning against one parent

These are general indicators that the child may be troubled—though not necessarily about sexual assault. However, if you can recognize some of these signs early, you may be able to prevent an assault from becoming more severe.

LIFESAVER EMERGENCY ALERT CARDS

Your local police can get free lifesaver cards to give to the children in your community. These very small cards are made of a special material that is virtually indestructible. They look like paper but cannot be ripped and once written on are permanent. They are tied to the child's shoes and worn between the laces and the tongue. Each card serves to:

1. Identify the child,
2. Provide medical information to paramedics and doctors,
3. Locate the parents through three emergency telephone numbers,
4. Locate the family doctor, which opens access to medical records and to confer by telephone with someone who knows the child.

These cards are more than just identification; they supply a lot of information and are easily accessible to emergency personnel even if your child is unconscious or lost.

8. Jennifer Fay, "*He Told Me Not to Tell* (King County Rape Relief, 305 S. 43rd, Renton, Wash. 98055, copyright 1979), 16. Used with permission.

Cards also can be obtained from the following nonprofit charity:

Lifesaver Charities
6950 Aragon Circle, Suite 5
Bueno Park, California 90620

A QUICK CHECK FOR YOUR CHILD'S SAFETY[9]

Do you have an identification file for each child?
Each file should include:
- Footprints and finger prints
- Birth certificate
- Full-face pictures (update four times a year)
- Dental records
- Medical records, including blood type, illnesses, X-rays
- Physical description: hair color, weight, height, eye color, and distinguishing characteristics
- Lock of hair
- Passport
- Tape recording of child's voice

Have you taught your children survival or safety skills?
Are you very cautious and do you check references for a new babysitter?
Do you ever leave your child unattended in a car?
Do you know your child's route to school and to friends' houses?
Can your child make a telephone call for help? to home? long distance?
Have you posted emergency telephone numbers near the telephone?
Have you taught your child his or her full name, address, and telephone number?
Do you have deadbolt locks and a peephole on your home doors?
Have you set up neighbors who are your child's second line of defense (a place to go to if bothered when walking or to telephone)?
Do you hold onto your child in a crowded area, shopping mall, carnival?
Do you request malls to employ security people who are visible and available for children to be able to approach if bothered?
Have you requested your local schools, police, and religious organizations to provide safety seminars on ways of protecting young children and seminars for the children themselves in awareness training?

---

9. These suggestions are based on the sheet entitled "Recommended Precautions" from: Friends of Child Find of Newton, 29 Fair Oaks Avenue, Newton, Massachusetts 02160; Tel. (617) 235–4145.

WHAT TO LOOK FOR IN A GOOD DAY-CARE CENTER OR PRESCHOOL PROGRAM

Most centers are good and well-staffed. For your sake and that of your child, however, you should check out any program *before* enrolling your child. Differences in philosophy and teaching styles may affect your child's happiness in a particular program. Choosing a day-care center or a preschool is an important decision that needs thought.

What Are Your Child-Care Options?

1. Family Day-Care: A small group of children are cared for by one person, usually in his or her home. At its best, this situation can provide a home atmosphere with all nurturing that a parent would want for an infant, toddler, or young child. The home should be bright, cheery, and be set up for children. Television viewing should be limited and interaction a crucial part of the day. Activities should involve and motivate the youngsters.
2. Group Day-Care Centers: A center is a popular approach to child care needs for toddlers and preschoolers. Groups can be as large as eighty children but be divided into smaller groups for activities and play during the day. Most group centers comply with local or state guidelines as to teacher-child staff ratio. Be sure the center you choose is licensed and in compliance with local codes and standards. There is a wide variety of center programs and philosophies.
3. Cooperatives: This kind of care is often used in an area in which a number of parents wish to work together to provide mutual day-care rather than pay for it at the going public or private rates. Colleges or religious organizations often offer this type of care. Cooperatives are often run on a point system to keep them fair. Some questions to ask include: Who is watching your child? Are there ground rules that are written and consistently applied? What is happening at the co-op for activities?
4. One-to-One Care: This is an increasingly popular option that some people, especially two-parent working families, find appealing. The concept of the English nanny is finding its way into the American home. This is costly, but your child is at home in familiar surroundings, and care is managed your way. College students are often part-time one-to-one caregivers. Relying on one person means that a parent has to be extremely careful in checking out the prospective caregiver, and both parties must understand and agree on the caregiving guidelines.

5. New Options: These include employer-supported day-care which is on-site. The working parents can see their children during lunch and share part of the day while working. Another option is flexitime work schedules, when two people share one job and often cover for each other sitting for the other's child.
6. Traditional Options: These include use of a friend or relative to baby-sit. This option is more difficult nowadays because so many friends and grandmas are working and grandparents often live a distance from their grandchildren.

What to Look for in a Safe and Well-Organized Program

1. Be sure it is *licensed!* Having a license means that the program meets at least some standards and that some government agency is watching it.
2. Check the *reputation!* Reputation is very important to good child-care centers. Many rely on word of mouth to promote and keep their program full of children. Always check this aspect.
3. Ask about *staff turnover!* A good program tends to keep good staff. You want your child to have a stable environment and to form personal attachments. You want a responsive staff to whom you and your child can relate. A constant staff turnover, especially at the director level, can be disruptive and disturbing to your child.
4. How is the *individual attention?* Do the staff have time to answer your child? Do they individualize for varying needs of children within the group? Do the teachers seem to be on top of the situation as a rule or are they rushed and harried?
5. Is there a *variety of activities?* A good program includes lots of interest areas, such as puppetry, dress-up area, blocks, puzzles, art projects, music and song, science, and social studies, as well as such physical development activities as movement, climbing, and outdoor play.
6. Are the *activities age-appropriate* and do they show an *understanding of normal child development?* Is the program pushing the child to do lots of table work or school-like paper work? Is the program restrictive and too demanding? A good program for young children reflects the children's need to be an active learner who moves and learns through participation not through lecture and passive methods.
7. Is the program *Fun?* A child-care center should be an exciting and fun place for children. It should be stimulating and motivating. Although most children go through periods of not wanting to leave a parent, a good pro-

gram involves the child and the separation anxieties usually lessen. If they keep increasing, you will want to find out why.

8. Is the *staff qualified?* Do you know about the people who will be caring for your child? You should. A good program tells you what their staff qualifications and experiences are.
9. Is the staff willing to accept *parent visits, suggestions, and involvement?* A good staff is more than willing to listen and share ideas with the parents and include them in various activities throughout the year.
10. Is the program an *open program?* Do you feel that you could drop in a little early and be welcome? Does it feel friendly and warm?
11. Is the staff *safety-oriented?* Do you have to provide written permission for anyone other than parents to take your child? Does the center know where your child is at all times? Is care taken to see that ambitious activities are carefully supervised? Are strangers allowed to wander near or in the school?
12. What is the *staff-child* ratio? A good ratio provides excellent coverage and protection for your child. A good ratio lessens the chances of accidents or harm coming to your child and will help with most of the other concerns expressed in this chapter.
13. Is the staff *emotionally responsive* to your child? With all the fears about abuse, it is easy to forget that young children *need* good touches and warm words to develop and learn to foster trust in their lives. Good touches are vital for good emotional development. A caring teacher or caregiver is an essential component for your child's well-being. Be sure that your teachers bend down to the child's level and listen to the child in positive ways. A good teacher gives valid and positive feedback.
14. Wht is the *discipline code?* Is it compatible with your own? It should never allow hitting or striking a child. It should never allow screaming, yelling, or swearing. A good discipline code provides for positive reinforcements for good behavior. Negative actions are not viewed as 'bad child' but should be negated as incorrect choices of behavior and the better choice discussed. Time out should be used only as a last resort and limited in its use. Redirection, distraction, and other methods have proved to be more effective in changing behavior than so-called traditional methods. The better choices have always been used by the better teachers.
15. Does the program *involve your child with the community?* Are there field trips, walks, and/or visits from community helpers? In center-based programs, these should be in evidence and at least some should be included in family-based and other types of programs. Language development and interest in the world are often stimulated by such activities.

In the end, the choice is the parents'. Make it the right choice for you and your child. Take the time to check and recheck. When you find the right program for you and your child, be supportive and work with the teachers to provide a strong, common base of love and learning for the child that is consistent and fully supportive of the child's total development: physical, emotional, academic, and child-oriented.

HOW TO CHOOSE GOOD MATERIALS ABOUT ABUSE AND CHILDREN

Many of the materials flooding the market in light of the recent publicity around child sexual abuse are good and valid. However, some are not so good and contain scanty or confused information about abuse. In an effort to make teaching about sexual abuse palatable to shocked adults, some books minimize and reduce the problem to a warning or emphasize the molester as complete stranger instead of the more likely danger of molester as friend or even relative. A few books even tell children that if someone is a friend of dad's or your pal, then the children can trust that person. It is important to create a nonthreatening atmosphere, but lying to the children or putting such a broad statement into their mind will neither make them safe nor give them peace of mind. This is true if a friend does approach or molest the child. In fact, this approach would probably reinforce the child's sense of guilt and hinder a positive solution.

Good material is *factual* without using stall tactics and fancy words to explain what is going on. Good materials are *simple* and *on the child's level.* Good materials rely on *common sense* and use a *realistic approach* to a given situation. Good materials also rely on *making the children feel their rights are important* and that they are *important and believable.* Good materials lay blame *where it belongs*—on the *perpetrator,* not the *victim.*

Examine materials carefully before you buy or use them. The materials need not be costly to be good.

There are many types of materials now available to help the educator plan a successful child safety program. Books for parents and teachers about health, abuse, and parenting are an important part of the training for adults involved with children. Books that are geared to the children themselves are very important as reinforcement resources for the child safety rules.

Audio-visual materials are film strips, films, videotapes, records, and cassettes. Many audio-visual materials are available for use with children. Some are excellent and some not. It is important to preview any audio-visual materials prior to use with the children. Even though most agencies that permit borrowing of their materials have screened and approved them, the materials still may not be appropriate for your particular group of children at a given stage of safety development.

The next few pages contain suggestions on books and materials. Other good resources also are available, but these give you a place to begin.

REVIEWS OF SOME RESOURCES FOR TEACHERS AND PARENTS

Safety Kids by Janeen Brady Published by Brite Enterprises, Inc.

This coloring book and tape with safety songs is an excellent parent tool to reinforce safety training. The children really respond to the songs and remember the safety rules that each song teaches.

It's OK, to Say No! by RGA Creation Published by Playmore, Inc./Waldman Publishing Corp.

This inexpensive coloring book is well done and serves as a reinforcement for the safety lessons about strangers and dangers. The sheets make excellent take-home worksheets for the parent and child to color together. It is very positive in its approach with the children. It is endorsed by the Children's Justice Foundation.

Never Say Yes to a Stranger by Susan Newman Published by Perigee Books/Putnam Publishing Group

This book contains excellent stories to read with young children for safety rules reinforcement. This book is designed to make the discussion of options easy.

Play Safe, Grow Safe, Feel Safe, Go Safe
Published by Golden Press

These inexpensive activity books involve the children with stickers and coloring activities that cover various areas of safety. They are excellent for the kindergarten and primary school–aged children.

First Things First designed by Barbara Balch and illustrated by Rebecca Archey
Published by Upjohn

This excellent first-aid booklet has splendid pictures. It is super for use with preschoolers and primary school–aged children. Also available is a checklist for the medicine cabinet. For free copies write to:

Upjohn
First Things First
Third Floor
99 Park Avenue
New York, New York 10016

Sexual Abuse: Alerting Children to the Danger Zones by Joy Berry
Abuse and Neglect: Alerting Children to the Danger Zones by Joy Berry
Kidnapping: Alerting Children to the Danger Zones by Joy Berry
Published by WORD, Educational Products Division, Waco, Texas 76796

All the books are well done and include helpful messages and information for the parent.

No More Secrets by Oralee Wachter   Published by Little, Brown and Company, Boston

This book is especially good for children in upper elementary school.

Exploring Our Emotions (T-755)
Exploring Our Emotions 2 (T-824)
Community Helpers (T-755)
Community Helpers (T-824)
Published by Trend Enterprises, Inc.

These poster series and accompanying teacher's guides are excellent for discussion starters about various emotions and about community workers. Each poster is brightly colored and clearly illustrated. The teacher's guides have some very useful curriculum ideas. Trend products are available through most school catalogs.

Parent Advisor Information Center

This series of booklets on various issues about safety is often provided free of charge at pediatricians' offices. Each booklet is written by a person knowledgeable in the subject matter. Each contains excellent information that is easily read. Some sample titles are:

Handling Home Emergencies by Barry Vinocur
A Summer Safety Guide by Sandy Jones
How to Childproof Your Home by Jean Caldwell

These booklets are available from:

13-30 Corporation
505 Market Street
Knoxville, Tennesee 37902

Chef Combo Kit from the New England Dairy Council

This excellent nutrition training kit contains recipes, puzzles, lesson plans, and food model cards. The motivator in this kit is a handmade puppet called

Chef Combo. The kit also contains parent handout sheets. Children love learning nutrition with the Chef. The kit is inexpensive and sometimes can be purchased at a reduced rate if the teacher attends a training class. Check with your local Dairy Council for more information.

National Committee for Prevention of Child Abuse

A yearly catalog is published from this valuable resource agency. The booklets available through the catalog are inexpensive but very well done. They are an excellent source of statistics about parenting issues and child abuse. For information, write to:

NCPCA
332 South Michigan Avenue
Suite 1250
Chicago, Illinois 60604-4352
(212)663-3520

Child Passenger Safety Resource Center

This resource center provides Buckle Up Bear coloring books and stickers and other safety materials free of charge. These are excellent motivating materials, especially for young children. They are good to send home for parent-child interaction. Materials are available in Spanish also. Write to:

CPSRC
600 Washington Street
Number 705
Boston, Massachusetts 02111
(617)727-2662

American Lung Association

This association offers free materials, posters, and brochures available in quantity to send home to parents about choking, asthma, and other child-related issues. Check local listing for address and telephone number.

American Automobile Association

This association offers free materials, posters, brochures, and booklets for use with children about traffic safety and seat belts. An excellent booklet series is available for the very young child. The booklets cover every aspect of traffic safety from the child's perspective. Check local listing for address and telephone number.

National Association for the Education of Young Children

There are many good pamphlets and brochures available through this resource. Some sample titles include:

"Parent Involvement in Education" (#135) by Alice S. Honig
"The American Family: Myth and Reality" (#132) by A. Eugene Howard
"A Guide To Discipline," revised (#302) by Jean Galambos Stone

Order the entire catalog from:

NAEYC
1834 Connecticut Avenue, N.W.
Washington, D.C. 20009

American Heart Association

This organization offers many excellent health-related materials. They also offer at a minimal cost the *Heart Treasure Chest,* which is a fantastic curriculum about health and the heart geared to young children. Check local listing for address and telephone number.

HOT LINE TELEPHONE NUMBERS

If you need an 800 telephone number but do not know where to find it, call 1-800-555-1212. The toll-free directory operator will give you the telephone number provided you know the appropriate agency or company name. The number also can often be found if you can provide the subject, for example, child abuse.

Alcoholism and Drug Abuse	1-800-ALCOHOL
Educational Grants	1-800-638-6700
Hearing Help Line	1-800-424-8576
Lead Paint Poisoning	1-800-532-8571
Parents Anonymous	1-800-882-1250
Parental Stress	1-800-632-8188
Poison Information	1-800-842-9211
Sexual Abuse	1-800-792-5200

The National Association for the Education of Young Children has a special 800 telephone number. It can be useful, but it is not a hot line. The number is 1-800-424-2460.

Keep this list and add to it as you find additional telephone numbers. This is a good resource that can be shared with parents.

AUDIO-VISUAL RESOURCES FOR THE TEACHER

Films and Filmstrips

"Child Abuse: It Shouldn't Hurt to Be a Kid" 27 minutes Federal/state guidelines

Source: AIMS MEDIA
6901 Woodley Avenue
Van Nuys, California 91406
rental or purchase

"Child Abuse and the Law" 27 minutes Focus: reporting and recognition of signs

Source: Perennial Educators
930 Pitner Avenue
Evanston, Illinois 60202
rental or purchase

"Child Abuse and Neglect: NEA Multimedia Training Program" by Cynthia Crosson Tower Includes filmstrips, cassettes, and booklets. Covers definitions, recognition, and reporting.

Source: NEA Professional Library
P.O. Box 509
West Haven, Connecticut 06516

"Child Sexual Abuse: What Your Child Should Know" PBS film series Separate segments for parents and for children—grades K–3

Source: Indiana University Audio-Visual Center
Bloomington, Indiana 47405

"Children in Peril" 22 minutes Tour of hospitals and treatment centers

Source: Guidance Associates
Communications Park
Box 1000
Mount Kisco, New York 10549

"Incest: The Victim Nobody Believes" 23 minutes Three women discuss their experiences with incest as children.

Source: MTI Teleprograms
108 Wilmot Road
Deerfield, Illinois 60015
rental or purchase

"No More Secrets" 13 minutes partly animated grades 1–5

Source: ODN
74 Varick Street
New York, New York 10013
rental or purchase

"Some Secrets Should Be Told" Excellent short film for use with even young children.

Source: Local chapter of the Society for the Prevention of Cruelty to Children. Check local telephone listing.

The MSPCC also has several other films and materials for loan, as well as speakers for parent groups.

"Talking Helps" 28 minutes Training film for using the childrens' film "No More Secrets"

Source: ODN
74 Varick Street
New York, New York 10013

"What Tadoo" 18 minutes grades K–3 Two puppets tell children what to do to protect themselves from child molesters.

Source: MTI Teleprograms
108 Wilmot Road
Deerfield, Illinois 60015
rental or purchase

"Who Do You Tell?" 11 minutes animated grades K–6

Source: MTI Teleprograms
108 Wilmot Road
Deerfield, Illinois 60015
rental or purchase

Videotapes

Strong Kids, Safe Kids with the Fonz from "Happy Days" or Henry Winkler

This cassette is available at no charge from many video stores as a public service. It runs a bit long for most young children, but the content is excellent. It covers all aspects of safety and does a particularly good job on sexual victimization prevention. I would recommend its use with school-aged children but break it up into several viewings for children under the age of six. Plan to borrow the tape a few times rather than try to cover all the material in one sitting. With preschoolers, plan to show it after some training so it is a reinforcement rather than the main teaching tool.

Police

Many local police units offer police officers to use as a resource. The safety officer usually has had some training in working with children and has available special robots, films, and materials that can only add to any school safety program. Police officers will often visit the school with materials and speak with the children. These visits are planned ahead of time so the teacher and the officer can discuss exactly what service from the officer is desired. Topics covered by the safety officer may include street safety, my friend the police officer, stranger dangers, drugs, and even bicycle safety.

Source: Check your local white pages for the nonemergency police telephone number.

Hospitals

Many hospitals recognize the benefits derived from children who have been prepared for the hospital experience and offer tours that often include health-related issues and can include some safety issues. Plan ahead and build your curriculum around such a trip. Many hospitals offer films.

Source: Check your local telephone listing for the volunteer department at your local hospital.

HEALTH AND SAFETY RESOURCES

The following organizations are involved with health and safety and provide information on their respective subject areas. The information is particularly helpful when organizing your curriculum for the children.

Adults Molested as Children United
P.O. Box 592
San Jose, California

American Academy of Pediatrics
1801 Hinman Avenue
Evanston, Illinois 60204

American Guidance Service
1-800-328-2560
Publishing company with many training programs.

American Humane Association
Children's Division
9725 E. Hampden Avenue
Denver, Colorado 80231

American Medical Association
Department of Health Education
535 North Dearborne Street
Chicago, Illinois 60610

American Public Health Association
1015 18th Street, N.W.
Washington, D.C. 20036

Center for Health Promotion and Education
1600 Clifton Road, N.E.
Atlanta, Georgia 30333

Central Massachusetts Camp Fire Council
36 Lancaster Street
Worcester, Massachusetts 01608
(617) 753-5398
Piloted the CAT program for child victimization prevention.

Children's Awareness Training
105 Merrick Street
Worcester, Massachusetts 01609

Child Find
29 Fair Oaks Avenue
Newton, Massachusetts 02160

Consumer Information Center
Department 44
Pueblo, Colorado 81009

FACES (Formerly Abused Children Emerging in Society)
Manchester Memorial Hospital
Child-Life Department
17 Hayes Street
Manchester, Connecticut 06040

Lifesaver Charities
6950 Aragon Circle
Suite 5
Bueno Park, California 90620
Offer emergency tags for children.

National Committee for Prevention of Child Abuse
332 South Michigan Avenue
Suite 1250
Chicago, Illinois 60604

NCCAN Child Abuse Clearinghouse
1600 Research Boulevard
Rockville, Maryland 20850

National Education Association
1201 16th Street
Washington, D.C.

Personal Safety Curriculum
Homemakers Service
P.O. Box 927
31 Trumbell Road
Northampton, Massachusetts 01601

Safety and Fitness Exchange, Inc.
541 Avenue of the Americas
New York, New York 10011

In addition to these resources, use local resources such as a pediatrician, school nurse, police officer, firefighter, ambulance driver, and so on, to enliven the classroom curriculum.

NATIONAL SOURCES OF SEXUAL ABUSE INFORMATION AND HELP

CHILDHELP USA
National Campaign for the Prevention of Child Abuse and Neglect
National Headquarters
Woodland Hills, California 91370

Coalition for Child Advocacy
P. O. Box 159
Bellingham, Washington 98227

Daughters and Sons United
P. O. Box 952
San Jose, California 95108

King County Rape Relief
305 South 43rd Street
Renton, Washington 98055

Maltreatment of Youth Project
Boys Town Center for Study of Youth Development
Boys Town, Nevada 68010

National Center for the Prevention and Treatment of Child Abuse and Neglect
1205 Oneida Street
Denver, Colorado 80220

National Center on Child Abuse and Neglect
Children's Bureau
U.S. Department of Health and Human Services
P. O. Box 1182
Washington, D.C. 20013

National Child Abuse Coalition
1125 15th Street, N.W.
Suite 300
Washington, D.C. 20005

Parents Anonymous
22330 Hawthorne Blvd.
Suite 208
Torrance, California 90505

In Addition:
You can look to your local chapters of United Way, Department of Social Services, Association for the Prevention of Cruelty to Children, Rape Crisis Centers, Public Health Department, School Nurses Associations, YWCA, YMCA, Scout or Campfire Councils, and counseling services. You can usually find a link to one of these organizations through the white pages. Often, a link with one agency

or program leads to finding the other programs in your area. Some offer speakers, brochures, and even training for sexual abuse prevention. Other good sources are colleges with early childhood education or elementary education programs. Children's hospitals also often have some type of program about abuse prevention.

LOCAL SOURCES OF HELP AND INFORMATION

Catholic Charities
Children's Friends Society
Citizen Resource Centers
Church and temple programs
Council for Children
Department of Education
Department of Mental Health
Department of Social Services
Family Health Clinics
HELP for Children
Jewish Family Services
Libraries
Office for Children
Rape Crisis Centers
Specific organizations: Easter Seals, Girl Scouts, Boy Scouts, YMCA, YWCA, Girls' Club, Boys' Club, Camp Fire Girls, and so on.
Society for the Prevention of Cruelty to Children

Check your local yellow and white pages for the telephone numbers of these and other local agencies.

QUESTIONS FOR REVIEW

1. Who is the primary influence over young children?
2. In today's child-care system, who is likely to be the second most influential person in the life of a young child?
3. How should teachers and parents view their roles to be most effective in supporting children?
4. How can teachers facilitate parent relations in a more positive way?
5. How can parents facilitate teacher relations in a positive way?
6. How would you characterize the change in attitudes toward young children within the area of legal or constitutional movements?
7. Are all fifty states coordinating their child care laws?
8. Explain the three-pronged attack on child abuse and neglect.
9. Who is Dr. T. Berry Brazelton?
10. What is the movement within the day-care and preschool community itself?
11. According to Rape Crisis figures, how many children are usually molested *before* a victimizer is brought to trial?
12. Explain why knowledge of child safety is superior to a lack of knowledge.
13. Name three ways that parents can bridge the communication gap with their children.
14. Name four tips for stress reduction for parents.
15. What are two ways that children can signal their need for help?
16. What is a lifesaver emergency card?
17. What should be included in a quick check safety file for a child?
18. Name the five most common child-care options.
19. What are six of the fifteen points to look for in a well-run and safe preschool or day-care program?

Bibliography

PUBLICATIONS

Abraham, Willard. *Parent Talk.* Scottsdale, Ariz.: Sunshine Press, n.d.

Allen, K. Eileen, and Betty Hart. *The Early Years: Arrangements for Learning.* Englewood Cliffs, N.J.: Prentice-Hall, 1984.

American National Red Cross. *Basic Aid Training.* American Red Cross, 1980.

American National Red Cross. *Standard First Aid and Personal Safety.* New York: Doubleday & Company, 1981.

Auerbach, Stevanne. *Choosing Child Care: A Guide for Parents.* New York: E. P. Dutton, 1981.

Baden, Genser, Levine, and Seligson. *School-Age Child Care, An Action Manual.* Boston: Auburn Publishing Company, 1982.

Biehler, Robert F. *Child Development: An Introduction.* Boston: Houghton-Mifflin, 1982.

Booher, Dianna Daniels. *Rape—What Would You Do If?* New York: Julian Messner, 1981.

Brazelton, T. Berry. *To Listen to a Child.* Reading, Mass.: Addison-Wesley Publishing Company, 1984.

Broman, Betty L. *The Early Years in Childhood Education.* Boston: Houghton-Mifflin, 1982.

Camarra, Muriel. "Parents and Children Growing Together." Citizen's Resource Center Workshop, University of Massachusetts Medical School. January 21, 1984.

Central Massachusetts Camp Fire, Worcester Rape Crisis, and Worcester Mental Health. *Children's Awareness Training.* Worcester, Mass., 1983.

Central Massachusetts Health Care, Inc. *Your Health and Fitness.* Highland Park, Ill.: Curriculum Innovations, June/July 1984.

Cook, Ruth E., and Virginia Armbruster. *Adapting Early Childhood Curricula: Suggestions for Meeting Special Needs.* St. Louis: C. V. Mosby Company, 1983.

Cottle, Thomas J. *Children's Secrets.* New York: Anchor Press, 1980.

Day, Barbara. *Early Childhood Education: Creative Learning Activities.* New York: Macmillan, 1983.

Dinkmeyer, Don, and Gary D. McKay. *The Parent's Handbook: STEP.* Circle Pines, Minn.: American Guidance Service, 1982.

Edwards, Jean, and Rebecca Harrison. *Child Abuse: A Personal Account and Guide for Teachers and Professionals.* Portland, Ore.: Ednick Communications, 1983.

Esse, Eva. *Practical Guide to Solving Preschool Behavior Problems.* Albany, N.Y.: Delmar Publishers, 1983.

Fay, Jennifer. "He Told Me Not To Tell." Renton, Wash.: King County Rape Relief, 1979.

Fernandez, Happy Cranven. *The Child Advocacy Book.* New York: Pilgrim Press, 1980.

Fields, Terri. "Teach Your Kids." *Family Circle* (March 6, 1984).

Flemming, Bonnie Mack, Hamilton, and Hicks. *Resources for Creative Teaching in Early Childhood Education.* New York: Harcourt, Brace and Jovanovich, 1977.

Garcia, Ricardo L. *Teaching in a Pluralistic Society.* New York: Harper and Row, 1982.

Grieff, Barrie, and Preston Munter. *Tradeoffs: Executive, Family and Organizational Life.* New York: Times Mirror, 1980.

Hall, Frances E., and Douglas T. Hall. *The Two Career Couple.* Reading, Mass.: Addison-Wesley, 1979.

Hibner, Dixie, and Liz Cromwell. *Finger Frolics.* Livonia, Mich.: Partner Press, 1980.

Hyde, margaret. *Cry Softly, the Story of Child Abuse.* Philadelphia: The Westminister Press, 1980.

Hyde, Margaret. *Sexual Abuse, Let's Talk about It.* Philadelphia: Westminister Press, 1984.

Kline, Donald F. *Child Abuse and Neglect: A Primer for School Personnel.* Reston, Va.: Council for Exceptional Children, 1977.

Long, Lynette, and Thomas Long. *The Handbook for Latchkey Children and Their Parents.* New York: Arbor House, 1983.

McHenry, Patrick, and Patsy Skeen. "The Teacher's Role in Facilitating the Child's Adjustment to Divorce." *Annual Editions: Early Childhood Education,* ed. Judy Spitler McKee. Guilford, Ct.: Dushkin Publishing Group, 1982.

Morgan, Rex. "Focus On: Dr. T. Berry Brazelton." *The Cable Guide* (June 1984).

Olds, Sally Wendkos. *The Working Parent's Survival Guide.* New York: Bantam Books, 1983.

Sanford, Linda Tschirthart. *Come Tell Me Right Away.* Lebanon, N.H.: New Victoria Printers, 1980.

Schaefer, Michael W. *Child Snatching.* New York: McGraw-Hill, 1984.

Squibb, Amy. "Growing Together Outside the Home." Citizen's Resource Center Workshop, University of Massachusetts Medical School, Worcester, Mass., January 21, 1984.

"Victim 9, On Rapist: Jail Him." *Evening Gazette,* Worcester, Mass. (May 2, 1984).

Warren, Jean, comp. *Piggyback Songs.* Everett, Wash.: Totline Press, 1983.

——— *More Piggyback Songs.* Everett, Wash.: Totline Press, 1984.

Wortham, Sue Clark. *Organizing Instruction in Early Childhood.* Newton, Mass., Allyn and Bacon, 1984.

OTHER RESOURCES

Nancy Biledeau, Child Advocate, Child Care Referral, United Way of Worcester, Mass.

Maureen Callan Binienda, Generic Specialist, Worcester Public Schools, Worcester, Mass.

Yvonne Lutter, Worcester Rape Crisis Center, Worcester, Mass.

John McFadden, Special Education, Worcester Public Schools, Worcester, Mass.

Raymond McGrath, Worcester Police Department, Worcester, Mass.

Local sources of resources for you may include police departments, fire departments, United Way services, rape crisis centers, school departments, hospitals, and the Department of Public Health.

INDEX

Address, teaching to children, 48–49, 116–17
Adult responsibilities, in child abuse cases, 160–61
Alcohol, 74
"Alive and Well," 177
American Automobile Association, 99, 114, 192
American Heart Association, 193
American Lung Association, 192
American Red Cross, 13, 48
Anger, expression of, 40–42
Appliances, hazards of, 78–79
Athletics, considerations for, 96–97
Audio-visual resources for teachers, 194–96
Automobile safety, 114–15

Bad touches, 137
Basic first aid, 47–52, 53–57 *fig.*, 58–59
BAT (Basic Aid Training) program, 13, 49
Blitz rape, 163
Body, learning about, 37–38
Body part names, 142, 143 *fig.*
Book making, 22
Brazelton, T. Berry, 177
Buddy system, 116
Bullies, 131–32

Camarra, Muriel, 8
Car safety, 114–15
Cereals, sugar in, 61–62, 62–63 *fig.*
Certificate samples, 29–31
Chef Combo Kit, 191–92
Child abuse, 176
Child care centers
  licensing of, 178–79
  options for, 186–87
  program guidelines, 187–89
Child development
  courses in, 173
  five-year-old, 3
  four-year-old, 2
  six-year-old, 4–5
  three-year-old, 1
Child labor, 176
Child neglect, indicators of, 162
Child Passenger Safety Resource Center, 192
Child-proof bottle caps, 72–73
Childproofing the home, 87–88
Children's Awareness Training (CAT), 24, 119
Children's Museum (Boston), 177–78
Children's rights, 36, 120, 166, 175–76
Christmas greens, 83
Colgate Company, 60
Common household poisons, 84
Communication, 174–75
Communication gap, ten ways to bridge, 181–82
Confidence rape, 163

Confusing touches, 137
Cookie cutter sandwiches, 67
Cooperatives (child care), 186
Council for Children, 178–79
Court testimony and children, 179–80
Crazy lunch, 67
Cruelty to Animals, Society for the Prevention of, 175
Custodial battles, 158

Dangers, 9–10
Day care, 11
  options for, 186–87
  program guidelines, 187–89
  safety rules for, 94–96
Dental care
  nutrition, 60–61
  nutritious snacks, 69
  snack activities, 66–68
  sugar content in foods, 61–65
  tooth activities, 66
Development. *See* Child development
Discipline code (sample), 183 *fig.*
Diving, 77
Divorce rate, 10
Dolls, 172
Door safety, 111–13
Driveway hazard, 82
Drug abuse, 159–60
  signs of, 165
Dyke, Dick van, 75

Education of Young Children, National Association for the, 178, 193
Emotions, expression of, 36, 38–42
Equipment guides (infant and toddler), 90–91

Fact sheets, 174
Family, 36
Family Circle Magazine, 177
Family day care, 186
Fears, of young children, 47–48
Feeling good
  body, learning about, 37–38
  emotions, 38–42
  family, 36
  individuality, 37
  objectives, 33–36
  personal space, 42–43, 44–45 *fig.*
  words and phrases for positive self-concepts, 44–45
Fieldman, Bruce S., 60
Films, 194–96
Filmstrips, 194–96
Fireplaces, 76
Fire safety, 74–76, 88–89 *fig.*
First aid handbook, 51, 53–57 *fig.*
First aid instruction, 13, 15–21 *fig.*
  basic first aid, 47–51, 52–57 *fig.*, 58–59
  dental care and nutrition, 60–69
First aid kit, 52 *fig.*, 59
First Things First (Balch), 190
Fish ka-bobs, 67
Five senses, 120, 121–28 *fig.*, 130
Five-year-old, 3
Flexitime work schedules, 187
Flossing, 60
Four-year-old, 2
Fruit juice pops, 67–68
Fruit ka-bobs, 67

Good touches, 137
Green light feelings, 137
Group day-care centers, 186

Hahnemann Hospital, 59
Halloween safety, 103–4
Hallucinogenics, 83
Happiness, 38–39
Hazards, in home, 80–82
Head swing technique, 153
Health and safety resources, 197–98
Home safety
  athletics, considerations for, 96–97
  childproofing the home, 87–88
  dangerous plants, 82–84
  equipment guides (infant and toddler), 90–91
  fire safety, 74–76, 88–89 *fig.*
  house safety tour, 80–82
  lead poisoning, 85–86, 86 *fig.*
  outdoor play equipment, 92
  outdoor playground, safety rules, 92–94
  poison, 71–74
  preschool and day care safety rules, 94–96
  toy safety, 91–92
  water safety, 77–78
Hospitals, 196
Hospital tours, 58–59

Hot line numbers, 193–94
Household items, hazards of, 78–79
House plants, poisonous, 83

Ice rescue, 78
Ice skating, 77–78
Incest, 163
Individuality, 37
Inhalants, 160
International Labor Organization, 176
It's OK to Say No!, 190

Ka-bob dips, 67
Kick technique, 151–53
Kidnapping, 115, 158–59
Kitchen stove, 76

Lead poisoning, 85–86, 86 *fig.*
Legal system, 175–76, 179–80
Licensing (child care centers), 178–79
Lifesaver cards, 184–85
Local sources of help and information, 199

Matches, 76
McMartin School case, 180
Memo board, 174
Mental Health Association, 161
Molesters, 155–58, 179
Mr. Yuk stickers, 74

National Fire Protection Association, 75
Native plants, poisonous, 83
Natural gas, 76
Neglect, indicators of, 162
Never Say Yes to a Stranger (Newman), 190
No game, 132
No More Secrets (Wachter), 191
Nutrition
  and nutritious snacks, 69
  and snack activities, 66–68
  and sugar in foods, 60–65

Older children, helping role of, 170–71
On-site day care, 187
One-to-one care, 186
Outdoor plants, poisonous, 83
Outdoor play equipment, 92
Outdoor playground, safety rules for, 92–94
Outer space saucers, 67

Painted bread, 67
Parent, teacher, community relations, 170–74
  audio-visual resources for teachers, 194–96
  child care programs, what to look for, 186–89
  children's rights, 175–76
  choosing materials about abuse, 189
  communication, 174–75
  communication gap, 10 ways to bridge, 181–82
  health and safety resources, 197–98
  hospitals, 196
  hot line numbers, 193–94
  licensing day care facilities, 178–79
  lifesaver cards, 184–85
  local sources of help and information, 199
  police, 196
  public relations and laws, 179–80
  reviews of resources for teachers and parents, 190–93
  safety check, 185
  safety education, 177–78, 180–81
  sexual abuse, national sources of information and help, 198–99
  time-out tips, 182, 183 *fig.*
  trouble indicators, 184
  videotapes, 196
Parent Advisor Information Center, 191
Parenting, 173–74
Parent's Magazine, 92
Passport, 159
Password concept, 108
Pediatric dentistry, 65
Personal space, 42–43, 44–45 *fig.*, 130
Physical abuse, indicators of, 162
Piaget, Jean, 11
Pickle alligators, 68
Piggyback Songs (Warren), 49
Pinwheel sandwiches, 67
Plants, dangerous, 82–84
Playground safety rules, 92–94
Play Safe, Grow Safe, Feel Safe, Go Safe, 190
Poison, 71–74
  common household poisons, 84
Poisonous plants, 82–84
Police, 196
Police and children, 113–14
Praise, 34
Preschool Children in Traffic, 99

Preschools
  program guidelines, 187
  safety rules for, 94–96
Prevention of Child Abuse, National Committee for, 192
Public relations, 179–80

Rape, 163
Reality, and children, 11–13
Red light feelings, 137
Resources for teachers and parents, reviews of, 190–93
Rights, of children, 36, 120, 166, 175–76
Role playing, 22, 107, 172

Sadness, 39
Safety curriculum, 7–9
  adult objectives, 27
  basic premises of, 25–26
  children and reality, 11–13
  content area objectives, 26–27
  first aid instruction, 13, 15–21 *fig.*
  safety, teaching methods for, 13, 22–25
  societal changes, effect of, 9–11
  teaching methods for, 13, 22–25
Safety education, 177–78
  need for, 180–81
Safety Kids (Brady), 190
Safety rhymes, 146–47 *fig.*
Safety tour, in home, 80–82
Sealants, 60
Seat belts, 114
Secrets, 134, 135 *fig.*
Self-concept, 33–34
  words and phrases for, 44–45
Self-defense, 151–55
Senses, 120, 121–28 *fig.*, 130
Sexual body parts, 38
Sexual misuse, 163
Sexual victimization, 135
  fact sheet on, 163–65
  indicators of, 162
  national sources of information and help, 198–99
  statistics on, 136
Sharing, 34–35
Single parenting, 10–11
Six-year-old, 4–5
Snack bugs, 66
Snacks, 61
  nutritious snacks, 69
  snack activities, 66–68
Social Security card, 158–59
Social Services, Department of, 161
Societal changes, 9–11
Sports, considerations for, 96–97
Sticker cards, 23, 28 *fig.*
Strangers, 155–58
  safety and, 104–11
Street smarts
  automobile safety, 114–15
  door safety, 111–13
  knowing addresses, 116–17
  knowing telephone numbers, 116
  police and children, 113–14
  stranger safety, 104–11, 115–16
  telephone safety, 111
  traffic safety, 99–104
  walking children, tips for, 117
Stress, 170
Sugar
  in cereals, 61, 62–63 *fig.*
  in foods, 64–65
Survival skills, 12
Swimming, 77–78

Talking, 34
Tattling *vs.* telling, 132, 133–34 *fig.*, 135
Teacher, role of, 173
Teddy bear, as teaching tool, 51
Teeth. *See* Dental care
Telephone numbers, teaching to children, 116
Telephone safety, 111
Telephone skills, 49–50
Three-year-old, 1
Time-out tips, 182, 183 *fig.*
Touch, 137, 138–41 *fig.*, 142, 143–44 *fig.*, 145
Toy safety, 91–92
Traffic safety, 99–104
Trouble indicators, 184
Turtle Magazine, 104
Typewriter fluid, 160

"Uncle Harry and Amy," 167–68

Vegetables and dip, 68
Victimization, 149

Victimization prevention, 119
  adult responsibilities, 160–61
  bullies, 131–32
  children's rights, 120, 166
  drug abuse, 159–60, 165
  five senses, awareness of, 120, 121–28 *fig.*, 130
  indicators of abuse and neglect, 162
  key words for parents, 166–67
  kidnapping, 158–59
  other senses, 130
  personal space, 130
  review activities, 145, 146–47 *fig.*, 148–49
  self-defense, 151–55
  sexual victimization, 135–37, 138–41 *fig.*, 142, 143–44 *fig.*, 145, 163–65
  stranger danger, 155–58
  tattling *vs.* telling, 132, 133–34 *fig.*, 135
  victimization, 149
  "Uncle Harry and Amy," 167–68
Videotapes, 196
Viscusi, W. Kip, 72

Walking children, tips for, 117
Water safety, 77–78
What Every Baby Knows, 177
Wild plants, poisonous, 83
Wood-burning stoves, 76
Working mothers, 11

Yell technique, 151